Learning to Walk
in the Dark

HarperOne Titles by Barbara Brown Taylor

Leaving Church: A Memoir of Faith
An Altar in the World: A Geography of Faith

Learning to Walk in the Dark

BARBARA BROWN TAYLOR

HarperOne
An Imprint of HarperCollinsPublishers

For all the children of the night

HarperOne

Grateful acknowledgment is given to the following publishers for permission
to reprint excerpts from the following copyrighted works:

The lines on page 91 from "To Know the Dark" by Wendell Berry are reprinted from *Selected Poems of Wendell Berry* copyright © 1998 Wendell Berry by permission of Counterpoint Press. The lines on page 133 from "Lost" by David Wagoner are reprinted from *Traveling Light: Collected and New Poems* copyright 1999 by David Wagoner with permission of the University of Illinois Press. The prayer by Thomas Merton between Chapter 9 and the Epilogue is reprinted from *Thoughts in Solitude* copyright 1956, 1958 by the Abbey of Our Lady of Gethsemani, published by Farrar, Straus and Giroux.

HarperCollins books may be purchased for educational, business, or sales promotional use. For information please e-mail the Special Markets Department at SPsales@harpercollins.com.

HarperCollins website: http://www.harpercollins.com

HarperCollins®, ■®, and HarperOne™ are trademarks of HarperCollins Publishers.

FIRST HARPERCOLLINS PAPERBACK EDITION PUBLISHED IN 2015

Interior Design by Laura Lind Design
Illustrations by Lydia Hess

Library of Congress Cataloging-in-Publication Data
Taylor, Barbara Brown.
Learning to walk in the dark / Barbara Brown Taylor. — first edition.
pages cm
Includes bibliographical references.
ISBN 978-0-06-202434-3
1. Spiritual life—Christianity. 2. Light—Religious aspects—Christianity. I. Title.
BV4509.5.T395 2014
248.4—dc23   2013027749

16 17 18 19 RRD(C) 10 9 8 7 6 5

There is a tendency for us to flee from the wild silence and the wild dark, to pack up our gods and hunker down behind city walls, to turn the gods into idols, to kowtow before them and approach their precincts only in the official robes of office. And when we are in the temples, then who will hear the voice crying in the wilderness? Who will hear the reed shaken by the wind?

—Chet Raymo, *The Soul of the Night*

CONTENTS

Introduction: Treasures of Darkness

I will give you the treasures of darkness and riches hidden
in secret places, so that you may know that it is I, the LORD,
the God of Israel, who call you by your name.

—Isaiah 45:3

Come inside now, it's getting dark." That is my mother speaking, saying the same thing she said every night when she looked out the kitchen window and saw that the sun was going down. It did not matter whether the window was in Kansas, Ohio, Alabama, or Georgia. Dark was dark, and she wanted her children inside. It must have cost her a lot to call us, since it meant that the quiet house would soon be filled with the noise of three small, loud girls, but she did it anyway. She loved us enough to let us play outside until the cicadas cranked up and bats started swooping through the sky; then she loved us enough to call us inside so that nothing bad would happen to us in the dark.

The dangerousness of the dark was like the law of gravity. No one could say exactly how it worked, but everyone agreed on it. When night fell, children were gathered inside, front porch lights were switched on, curtains were drawn, and doors were locked. The inside of the house became a showcase of artificial light: the fluorescent ring on the ceiling of the kitchen, 40-watt appliance bulbs in the oven hood, 25-watt bulbs shaped like candles in the dining room chandelier, standard 60-watt bulbs in the lamps in the living room, the phosphorescent glow of the television set in the den. There was nothing you could not do in a house like that. Even if you got up in the middle of the night to go to the bathroom, small night-lights plugged into every baseboard outlet would guide you to your destination like an airplane making a landing after dark.

I never questioned the need for all this light, since the dangerousness of the dark was more apparent to me inside the house than out. After one or the other of my parents had kissed me good night and turned off the light by my bed, there was always a moment of bliss under the tent of my sheets while my eyes adjusted to the low light coming through the window. Had I been an easy sleeper, I might have drifted off on that tide of contentment, but I have never been an easy sleeper.

Once the smell of my parents had faded away along with their footsteps; once I could feel their protection dissipate as they moved away from me; once it became apparent to me that they had checked me off their list for the night and had turned their attention to other things, then all the loose darkness in that room started to collect in the closet and under the bed, pulling itself together with such magnetic malevolence that I could not keep my mind away from it.

Without benefit of maturity or therapy, I had no way of knowing that the darkness was as much inside me as it was outside me, or that I had any power to affect its hold on me. No one had ever taught me to talk back to the dark or even to breathe into it. The idea that it might be friendly was absurd. The only strategy I had ever been taught for dealing with my fear of the dark was to turn on the lights and yell for help. Even then, when my parents came back to ask what I was afraid of, they took my answers at face value. "There are no monsters under your bed," they assured me, getting down on their knees to look. "There are no witches in your closet," they said, opening the door to show me, as if scientific proof would make a bit of difference once they had turned out the lights and left the room again.

Since I am only five years old in this memory, there is no telling what I might have said if they had asked me what color the monsters' eyes were, or what the witches were planning to do to me. If they had, I might have learned to become more curious about what the darkness inside me was dishing up. I might have learned to look more deeply instead of looking away, but one thing my parents and I shared was the wish for a quick fix. They wanted to get back to whatever they were doing in the living room and I wanted to stop being afraid, so we settled on a solution that worked for both of us: eliminate the darkness. Leave a light on in my room at night so that it was never dark.

You would have to ask an anthropologist how well this childhood history matches the history of the human race, but when I look around the world today, it seems clear that eliminating darkness is pretty high on the human agenda—not just physical darkness but also metaphysical darkness, which includes psychological, emotional, relational, and spiritual darkness. What do I mean by "darkness"? I guess that depends on what color your monsters' eyes are. Most people do not know what they mean by "darkness" except that they want to stay out of it. Just say the word and the associations begin to flow: night, nightmare, ghost, graveyard, cave, bat, vampire, death, devil, evil, criminal, danger, doubt, depression, loss, fear. Fear is the main thing. Almost everyone is afraid of being afraid. Beyond that, no one's list is exactly like anyone else's. It fits the way a shadow fits, because darkness is sticky. It attracts meaning like a magnet, picking up everything in its vicinity that is not fully lit.

If you decide to read the rest of this book, you will learn plenty about what darkness means to me. For now, it is enough to say that "darkness" is shorthand for anything that scares me—that I want no part of—either because I am sure that I do not have the resources to survive it or because I do not want to find out. The absence of God is in there, along with the fear of dementia and the loss of those nearest and dearest to me. So is the melting of polar ice caps, the suffering of children, and the nagging question of what it will feel like to die. If I had my way, I would eliminate everything from chronic back pain to the fear of the devil from my life and the lives of those I love—if I could just find the right night-lights to leave on.

At least I think I would. The problem is this: when, despite all my best efforts, the lights have gone off in my life (literally or figuratively, take your pick), plunging me into the kind of darkness that turns my knees to water, nonetheless I have not died. The monsters have not dragged me out of bed and taken me back to their lair. The witches have not turned me into a bat. Instead, I have learned things in the dark that I could never have learned in the light, things that have saved my life over and over again, so that there is really only one logical conclusion. I need darkness as much as I need light.

The problem is that there are so few people who can teach me about that. Most of the books on the *New York Times* "How-To" bestseller list are about how to avoid various kinds of darkness. If you want to learn how to be happy and stay that way, how to win out over your adversaries at work, or how to avoid aging by eating the right foods, there is a book for you. If you are not a reader, you can always find someone on the radio, the television, or the web who will tell you about the latest strategy for staying out of your dark places, or at least distract you from them for a while. Most of us own so many electronic gadgets that there is always a light box within reach when any kind of darkness begins to descend on us. Why watch the sun go down when you could watch the news instead? Why lie awake at night when a couple of rounds of Moonlight Mahjong could put you back to sleep?

I wish I could turn to the church for help, but so many congregations are preoccupied with keeping the lights on right now that the last thing they want to talk about is how to befriend the dark. Plus, Christianity has never had anything nice to say about darkness. From earliest times, Christians have used "darkness" as a synonym for sin, ignorance, spiritual blindness, and death. Visit almost any church and you can still hear it used that way today: *Deliver us, O Lord, from the powers of darkness. Shine into our hearts the brightness of your Holy Spirit, and protect us from all perils and dangers of the night.*

Since I live on a farm where the lights can go out for days at a time, this language works at a practical level. When it is twenty degrees outside at midnight and tree branches heavy with ice are crashing to the ground around your house, it makes all kinds of sense to pray for protection from the dangers of the night. When coyotes show up in the yard after dark, eyeing your crippled old retriever as potential fast food, the perils of the night are more than theoretical. So I can understand how people who lived before the advent of electricity—

who sometimes spent fourteen hours in the dark without the benefit of so much as a flashlight—might have become sensitive to the powers of darkness, asking God for deliverance in the form of bright morning light.

At the theological level, however, this language creates all sorts of problems. It divides every day in two, pitting the light part against the dark part. It tucks all the sinister stuff into the dark part, identifying God with the sunny part and leaving you to deal with the rest on your own time. It implies things about dark-skinned people and sight-impaired people that are not true. Worst of all, it offers people of faith a giant closet in which they can store everything that threatens or frightens them without thinking too much about those things. It rewards them for their unconsciousness, offering spiritual justification for turning away from those things, for "God is light and in him there is no darkness at all" (1 John 1:5).

To embrace that teaching and others like it at face value can result in a kind of spirituality that deals with darkness by denying its existence or at least depriving it of any meaningful attention. I call it "full solar spirituality," since it focuses on staying in the light of God around the clock, both absorbing and reflecting the sunny side of faith. You can usually recognize a full solar church by its emphasis on the benefits of faith, which include a sure sense of God's presence, certainty of belief, divine guidance in all things, and reliable answers to prayer. Members strive to be positive in attitude, firm in conviction, helpful in relationship, and unwavering in faith. This sounds like heaven on earth. Who would not like to dwell in God's light 24/7?

If you have ever belonged to such a community, however, you may have discovered that the trouble starts when darkness falls on your life, which can happen in any number of unsurprising ways: you lose your job, your marriage falls apart, your child acts out in some attention-getting way, you pray hard for something that does not happen, you begin to doubt some of the things you have been taught about what the Bible says. The first time you speak of these things in a full solar church, you can usually get a hearing. Continue to speak of them and you may be reminded that God will not let you be tested beyond your strength. All that is required of you is to have faith. If you still do not get the message, sooner or later it will be made explicit for you: the darkness is your own fault, because you do not have enough faith.

Having been on the receiving end of this verdict more than once, I do not think it is as mean as it sounds. The people who said it seemed genuinely to care about me. They had honestly offered me the best they had. Since their sunny spirituality had not given them many skills for operating in the dark, I had simply exhausted their resources. They could not enter the dark without putting their own faith at risk, so they did the best they could. They stood where I could still hear them and begged me to come back into the light.

If I could have, I would have. There are days when I would give anything to share their vision of the world and their ability to navigate it safely, but my spiritual gifts do not seem to include the gift of solar spirituality. Instead, I have been given the gift of lunar spirituality, in which the divine light available to me waxes and wanes with the season. When I go out on my porch at night, the moon never looks the same way twice. Some nights it is as round and bright as a headlight; other nights it is thinner than the sickle hanging in my garage. Some nights it is high in the sky, and other nights low over the mountains. Some nights it is altogether gone, leaving a vast web of stars that are brighter in its absence. All in all, the moon is a truer mirror for my soul than the sun that looks the same way every day.

After I stopped thinking that all these fluctuations meant something was wrong with me, a great curiosity opened up: what would my life with God look like if I trusted this rhythm instead of opposing it? What was I afraid of, exactly, and how much was I missing by reaching reflexively for the lights? Did I have enough faith to explore the dark instead of using faith to bar all my doors? How much more was in store for me if I could learn to walk in the dark? This book is a record of where I looked and what I found, which makes it more a journal than a manual. You are still welcome to come along, especially if you too have noticed phases in the brightness of your soul.

If you and I do not know one another, it may help you to know that I have spent half of my life as a priest in the Episcopal Church. I was ordained in my early thirties and served a couple of churches until I was close to fifty. Then I decided to leave parish ministry for a whole host of reasons, including my loss of faith in the institution I was serving. By writing a book about that experience, I discovered my part in my lover's quarrel with the church. Let's just say that an introverted romantic with a touch of obsessive-compulsive disorder does not make the best pastor. But I also discovered a number of things about my Christian tradition that had not been apparent to me while I was busy upholding it.

Chief among these is the way Christian teaching thrives on dividing reality into opposed pairs: good/evil, church/world, spirit/flesh, sacred/profane, light/dark. Even if you are not Christian, it should be easy to tell which half of each pair is "higher" and which "lower." In every case, the language of opposition works by placing half of reality closer to God and the other half farther away. This not only simplifies life for people who do not want to spend a lot of time thinking about whether the divisions really hold; it also offers them a strong sense of purpose by giving them daily battles to engage in. The more they win out over the world of the flesh, the better. The more they beat back the powers of darkness, the closer they get to God. The ultimate goal is to live with that God forever, in a bright heaven where the bottom half of every earthly equation has finally returned to dust.

After years of using this language to pray, teach, preach, and celebrate the sacraments, I fell out of love with it—not just the words themselves but also the vision of reality they represent. It was a huge loss, as full of grief as any other. The language had come as such blessed relief at first, naming the tug-of-war going on both inside and outside me. Why did I often feel so uncomfortable in my skin? Why did I do things that I knew were wrong? Earlier in my life, questions like these kept me up at night wondering what was wrong with me. When Christian teaching offered me an answer—that I was caught up in the fundamental struggle between spirit and flesh—it also offered me a strategy for victory. If I would commit myself to following Jesus, then every day, in every way, he would help me turn from the dark to live with him in the light.

Of course, my language evolved through the years as I became more mature in faith, but the essential worldview did not change. Even after I found a church that affirms the goodness of creation as much as any I know, Sunday worship still turned on the axis of blood sacrifice, which made the death of the body the way of eternal life. After I became ordained, I led the congregation in achingly beautiful prayers thanking God for the gifts of the earth, the church, and the Spirit—but also in prayers asking God to deliver us from the deceits of the world, the flesh, and the devil. Since this language matched much of the language in scripture, it blended in. Plus, it seemed to work for a lot of people, the same way it had worked for me.

It was not until later, after I had resigned from saying these words on a regular basis, that they began to sound lame. Their explanation for what was wrong with me was no longer a relief but an ongoing source of injury. Their description of divine reality no longer struck with the force of revelation but resounded with the clang of a truth claim that bore closer inspection. Saying them over and over again in a sacred place, it had been possible to overlook the way they divided people in two, teaching us over and over again that we had two minds, two natures, two sets of loyalties, two homes—and that only one was close to God. Too much of this can make a person crazy.

So I wrote a book in which I focused on spiritual practices rooted in ordinary, physical, human life on earth, like going for a walk, paying attention to a tree, hanging a load of laundry on the line, and treating other people like peepholes into God. This is how I learned that people of faith do not get much help in thinking of their ordinary, physical lives as being particularly sacred. All you have to do to get a thank-you note from some of them is to set down in print what they have known all along: that the days of their lives are not easily divisible into good and evil, spirit and flesh; that some of the best things that have ever happened to them have happened in the darkest places, and some of the worst in well-lit churches; that their bodies have been the source not only of great pain but also of great pleasure; that they experience the world as a place of wonder as well as brokenness; and that they have a hard time warming up to any kind of salvation that divides reality in two and asks them to forsake the bottom half.

In many ways this book is the third in a trilogy dedicated to scooping up the bottom halves of things, or at least the words used to describe them—first the world, then the flesh, now the dark—not only because those words have been libeled long enough but also because there is so much life in them that has been rejected on bogus grounds. If there is any truth to the teaching that spiritual reality is divided into halves, it is the truth that those pairs exist in balance, not opposition. What can light possibly mean without dark? Who knows spirit without also knowing flesh? Is anyone altogether good or altogether evil? Where is the church that exists outside the world? People of faith who are committed to fullness of life have our work cut out for us, if only in changing the way we talk.

This book is called *Learning to Walk in the Dark* because I believe that is a spiritual skill some of us could use right now. As I said earlier, "darkness" packs a different punch for different people. I do not know a thing about the darkness of living with chronic illness or trying to raise a child in a refugee camp, for instance. My eyes work well enough. I have never been sexually abused. All in all, my experience of physical darkness does not extend much beyond reading a good book by bad light. If I have any expertise, it is in the realm of spiritual darkness: fear of the unknown, familiarity with divine absence, mistrust of conventional wisdom, suspicion of religious comforters, keen awareness of the limits of all language about God and at the same time shame over my inability to speak of God without a thousand qualifiers, doubt about the health of my soul, and barely suppressed contempt for those who have no such qualms. These are the areas of my proficiency.

If even one of them rings a bell, it is possible that you too could benefit from learning to walk in the dark. Maybe you are a young person in deep need of faith right now, but the kind you inherited from your parents is not cutting it. You want something with a sharper edge, a keener sense of purpose. You want something that asks more of you than to sit and listen quietly while someone else tells you how to live. You know it's out there, but where? It may be time for a walk in the dark.

If you are in the middle of your life, maybe some of your dreams of God have died hard under the weight of your experience. You have knocked on doors that have not opened. You have asked for bread and been given a stone. The job that once defined you has lost its meaning; the relationships that once sustained you have changed or come to their natural ends. It is time to reinvent everything from your work life to your love life to your life with God—only how are you supposed to do that exactly, and where will the wisdom come from? Not from a weekend workshop. It may be time for a walk in the dark.

If you are my age, you are losing a lot more things than you once did—not just your keys and your vision, but also your landmarks and your sense of self. You are going to a lot more funerals now than before. When you read your class notes in the alumni news, they are shorter and nearer the top every time. You know full well where all this is heading, but you also know that you are not ready yet. So how are you supposed to get ready? What is the work you have left to do before you enter the Great Beyond? Clearly, it is time for a walk in the dark.

Since I have spent at least half my life in churches, I am especially aware of how many old-time Christians are looking into the dark right now. Attendance is down; debt is up. Plenty of smaller churches are closing or at least putting their buildings up for sale. All the divine energy seems to be going to the southern hemisphere, leaving the old-timers up north with a bad case of solar affective disorder. Learning to walk in the dark is an especially valuable skill in times like these—or maybe I should say *remembering* how to walk in the dark, since people of faith have deep pockets of wisdom about how to live through long nights in the wilderness. We just forgot, most of us, once we got where we were going and the glory days began.

The remembering takes time, like straightening a bent leg and waiting for the feeling to return. This cannot be rushed, no matter how badly you want to get where you are going. Step 1 of learning to walk in the dark is to give up running the show. Next you sign the waiver that allows you to bump into some things that may frighten you at first. Finally you ask darkness to teach you what you need to know. If you have never had a spiritual director before, you have started near the top. Let this one guide you, and you will soon have new companions as brave and curious as you are about the nightlife of your soul.

Meanwhile, here is some good news you can use: even when light fades and darkness falls—as it does every single day, in every single life—God does not turn the world over to some other deity. Even when you cannot see where you are going and no one answers when you call, this is not sufficient proof that you are alone. There is a divine presence that transcends all your ideas about it, along with all your language for calling it to your aid, which is not above using darkness as the wrecking ball that brings all your false gods down—but whether you decide to trust the witness of those who have gone before you, or you decide to do whatever it takes to become a witness yourself, here is the testimony of faith: darkness is not dark to God; the night is as bright as the day.

Since this is a book about learning to walk in the dark, the structure may sometimes be hard to see. The chapters track the phases of the moon, starting and ending with full moons. In between, the path winds, as the moon empties of light. Then, after a chapter on nights with no moon, the light begins to grow again. Once I decided to explore lunar spirituality, I resolved to follow darkness wherever it led, which is why this book has cosmology, biology, and psychology in it as well as history and theology. Anything that added to my wisdom about the human experience of darkness made it in, since that experience accounts for what we both love and fear about the night. Readers are free to take the science at face value, though I confess to taking much of it figuratively. Once, when I stood at the entrance of a very large labyrinth in a very old cathedral, my guide said, "From this point on, everything that happens is a metaphor for your life." Perhaps you will accept what follows in the same spirit. Whatever I meant to put into these pages, what you take from them is a metaphor for your life.

I have never written a book I have been sadder to finish, since I have enjoyed the writing of it so much. My consolation is knowing that I can walk out on my porch tonight and see the moon—one day past full—shining down on me like another mother, saying, "Come outside now, it's getting dark."

Who's Afraid of the Dark?

Whoever you are: some evening take a step
out of your house, which you know so well.
Enormous space is near.
—Rainer Maria Rilke

It is late August. I am lying in my yard on a blow-up mattress waiting for Friday to become Friday night, which is how I know people are wrong when they say, "It's as clear as the difference between night and day." That might be true at noon or midnight, but here at the liquid edge between day and night, the difference is so unclear that there are many words for it: sundown, twilight, nightfall, dusk. When I sit up for a better look, the mattress hisses like a rubber raft drifting on eventide. According to the rabbis, the Sabbath begins when three stars are visible in the sky, in which case I am not there yet. As it turns out, there is a lot of ground to cover between one sunset and three stars.

I am here to begin my study of darkness with the real thing, paying attention to it the way an artist or an astronomer might, instead of using it to gauge how much more I can get done before bed. Most nights sundown is useful only insofar as it tells me that the horses are stamping their feet at the pasture gate waiting to be fed. Once they and the three dogs have emptied their buckets and bowls, it is back to the kitchen to make supper, sort through the debris that collects on every flat surface during the upheavals of an ordinary day, start a load of laundry, and maybe watch an old episode of *West Wing* or *Grey's Anatomy* before settling down with a good book until the words run together and sleep puts the lights out.

Some nights the distractions are so plentiful that I do not even know what phase the moon is in, which was the whole point of moving to the country in the first place. When my husband Ed and I lived in the city, we almost never looked at the sky. When we were in the car, we looked at traffic. When we were on foot, we looked at the sidewalk while we talked about work, the weekend, and the kids. There was little reason to look up, since the night sky was almost always the same color. The reflective dome over the city took all the light that came its way, mixed it up, and painted the sky a metallic taupe that admitted few heavenly bodies. Even when the moon was full, it was hard to get a glimpse of it between the tall buildings that ringed the city in every direction.

One night, on our evening walk, we decided to haul anchor and move someplace where we could be on more intimate terms with the moon in all her seasons. If this does not sound important to you, I am not sure I can explain it. It had something to do with the growing awareness that our own seasons were numbered and we did not have forever to start paying attention to them. Plus, there is something promising in the cycles of the moon—now you see her, now you don't— for those who are more than halfway through what feels for all the world like a linear life with a period in view.

I took a cut in pay when I moved to the country, but the sky alone is worth it. Tonight, for instance, I am lying on a circle of flagstones still warm from the day's sun. The house is right behind me, at the top of a small hill. In front of me the view opens in every direction, with the hill falling away into darkness and the silhouette of a big bald-faced mountain dominating the horizon. There are no other dwellings visible in any direction, which means that there are no house lights, porch lights, security lights, or headlights to compete with whatever is about to show up in the sky.

The sky over my head has changed from blue to saffron to an inky plum color, which the thin gray clouds on the horizon are soaking up like cloths dropped on a spill. The air is not cool yet, but it is cooling fast. The light cotton sheet I have thrown over my legs is starting to feel damp. Dew is condensing on my upper lip. Above my head, a single bat is making loop de loops as it hones in on hapless insects and plucks them from the air. If the rabbis had said that the Sabbath begins when you see three bats in the sky, then I would be a third of the way there—but there are still no stars in the sky. I thought I saw one a minute ago, but when I blinked it was gone.

During the day it is hard to remember that all the stars in the sky are out there all the time, even when I am too blinded by the sun to see them. While I am driving to the post office to pick up my mail, a shooting star could be flying right over the hood of my car. While I am walking to the library to return an overdue book, Orion's Belt could be twinkling right above me. It is always night somewhere, giving people the darkness they need to see, feel, and think things that hide out during the day.

Since literal darkness is both the trigger and the metaphor for almost all the other kinds, this seems like the place to start. There is so much folklore about darkness, so much baggage packed by people whose hopes and fears are far different from mine, that it seems important to pay attention to the arrival of it for once, letting curiosity take the place of evasion. Even if it is just for one night, what can I learn about darkness by lying in wait for it like this?

According to the U.S. Naval Observatory, every day ends with three different twilights. Civil twilight begins a little before dark, when you first notice that it is time to use the headlights on your car. For some, this realization does not come until the last three approaching cars have blinked their headlights at you. Mild confusion ensues—did you leave your pocketbook on top of the car *again*?—until the brain puts dark and dark together and turns the headlights on.

Civil twilight is over by the time I take up my post in the yard. The moon is at half-mast, lying low over the darkening horizon. It will be full tonight—what the first people who lived here called a Grain Moon since the hay in the field is ripening for the second time this summer. The sky still has enough light in it that every now and then I see something that looks like a miniature biplane flying past—either a dragonfly or a pair of insects into adventurous sex. The bat has apparently called it a night.

Nautical twilight comes next, when the brightest stars are visible enough to steer by. That means Venus will be a front-runner, showing up low over the western horizon while the cicadas kick up their chorus of thrumming in the woods. There are fewer crickets tonight, but they send their messages too, along with a pair of night birds trying to find each other in the dark. When the compressor for the air conditioning in the house turns on, I feel apologetic. I had no idea how loud it was out here, clearly interrupting a whole valley full of creatures that are trying to say something to one another.

Above all our heads, the arrival of nautical twilight is not looking good. The thin gray blanket of clouds has grown, covering the moon along with the rest of the sky. What do people do, on nights like this, in countries where the start of a festival or a month of fasting depends on a clear view of the moon? Every now and then it shows through the clouds that are moving across its face. One moment it looks like the eye of a hawk in profile. The next it looks like the eye at the top of the pyramid on a dollar bill. Why does it never look simply like the moon behind clouds? I do not know. All I know is that I never tire of pulling the moon to earth by likening it to something I know down here.

When the thickening clouds leave no doubt that nautical twilight will not be happening tonight—much less astronomical twilight, which begins when even the faintest stars are visible—I think that I should go inside, but I do not go inside. The sky changes every couple of seconds. The breeze is slight but delectable. The sounds come from all directions at once. If I put out my hand to touch the flagstones beneath my raft, I can still feel the heat of the day in them, as if the earth were a sleeping animal giving off warmth.

To go inside would be like putting down a glass of cool spring water to go drink a store-brand cola. It would be like blowing out a pearl-colored candle to go read by a compact fluorescent light. Why would someone do that? The only reason I can think of is because she does not know what to do with so much night, especially since nothing she can do in it counts as productive, useful, or even moderately aerobic.

This struggle goes on for about twenty more minutes before productivity wins out. Rolling off my raft, I stand and fold the cotton sheet, dragging the mattress up to the porch behind me. Then I say good night to the moon and go inside the house to deal with the detritus of my day.

Later, lying in my bed, I feel cut off from everything that is going on outside my windows. I feel too loose, like a baby who has been unwound from her swaddling clothes and does not know what to do with her limbs. Outside, the gentle weight of the night had put me in my place and held me there, so that I could not ignore the spectacle of an ordinary summer evening. On a night like this, it is hard to understand why anyone would choose a reading lamp and the hum of the air conditioner over a box seat at the sound-and-light show outside, where it is always opening night.

My dog Dancer never makes that mistake. He has a bed inside too, but he would rather be outside—no matter what time it is, no matter how cold. Even if it is raining, he would rather be in the real dark than the artificial light. The only time he hangs on the porch is when the coyotes come close at night. Dancer can smell them before he sees their shadows in the pasture, where they prowl for rabbits or baby deer. They would be happy to eat Dancer's food if they could get close enough to do it, but then the wind shifts and they can smell him too. This sends them bounding back into the woods, yipping as they go, while Dancer lunges and snaps at the darkness from the top step of the porch. Then he points his muzzle straight at the moon and lets out a high howl unlike any other sound he makes. In seconds all the other dogs who hear him join in, letting the coyotes know that the neighborhood watch system is working. But as hard as they try to sound like coyotes, they cannot do it. Maybe it is because their throats are made differently, or maybe they are just too well fed. There is no other sound like the sound of a hungry coyote.

This train of thought cures me of the wish to be outside. I fall asleep to the white noise of the air conditioner and wake ready to get to work on darkness. There are all sorts of books to read, on astronomy, mythology, psychology, and theology, but the most important work is the kind no one else can do for me. I need to start taking some walks in my own dark.

When I first began telling people that I was studying darkness, their reactions all came from the same direction.

"That makes the hair stand up on the back of my neck," one woman said, rubbing the goose bumps that had sprung up on her arms.

"Is it about spiritual warfare?" someone else wanted to know.

"Darkness as in evil or darkness as in depression?" another asked.

Their associations with darkness were so uniformly negative that I thought about sending out a survey to discover how that had happened. How had so many people arrived at the conclusion that darkness was something to be feared, fought, gotten through, or avoided? Was it a Hollywood thing or a Freudian thing, a ghost story thing or a religious thing? Had their parents instilled the fear of darkness in them to keep them safe when they were young or did they have their own alarming experiences of the dark to fuel their fear? What explained their apparently universal agreement that the best way to deal with any kind of darkness was to turn on a light? There was no way to know without asking every one of them, so I did the next best thing. I reconstructed my own history with darkness.

As best I can remember, my parents did not teach me to fear the dark. Of course, I was born in the middle of the past century, when most middle-class families owned one car and watched one television at night. When there was nothing good on *Ed Sullivan* or *Lawrence Welk*, my father would take my sisters and me out into the backyard, where we would lie on our backs without talking and watch for falling stars. On the rare nights when we heard the siren of a fire engine nearby, he would bundle us in the car to chase the truck. With a little luck, we might spend the next few hours wrapped in blankets watching firefighters rout the orange flames shooting from the windows of an old barn or house. Our parents also took us camping a lot, so we learned not to get our sleeping bags in a knot every time a screech owl let loose or a raccoon came shuffling through the underbrush to eat the scraps of our supper.

When we lived in Tuscaloosa, Alabama, we bought a blue sixteen-foot Chris-Craft ski boat with a 25-horsepower Evinrude outboard motor. Our best friends, the Siegels, who also had three children, bought the same boat in red. After that we spent weekends on the Black Warrior River, camping at Deer Lick Campground for one or both nights. The Siegels slept in tents so they could camp anywhere, but the Browns slept in Army surplus jungle hammocks, so we needed a site with lots of trees. After we had found side-by-side lots that would work, we burned the stub end of our energy stringing the hammocks and laying a fire before dark.

The rest of the evening proceeded by smell: pork and beans flavored with ketchup cooking over the fire, paper plates burning in the same flames after dinner, charred sticks with blistered marshmallows on them, pinesap up close and river water farther away, arriving on the breeze with the smell of fish both living and dead. On warm evenings we headed back to the river after dark, the adults scandalizing the children by leaving their clothes on the dock and diving into the water with nothing on.

They did not need to tell us to leave them alone. The idea of our naked parents in the muddy river was so repellent to us that we would not have gone near the water for anything. All we could see from the shore were pale shapes circling each other in the dark water, calling out occasionally to make sure we were still there. Like the skinny-dipping adults, my sexuality floated just below the surface of my consciousness in those days, half in and half out. Although it was the nakedness and not the darkness that was most disturbing to me, the two got all mixed up in my mind.

After the adults had returned to normal, we gathered around the fire to listen to one of them tell a ghost story or read one from Edgar Allen Poe. My sisters and I lay with our heads in our parents' laps while the Siegel boys held flashlights

under their chins so that their noses cast gruesome shadows on their faces. We all knew how the stories ended, but
they sounded different in the dark. The malevolence in them
dripped to the ground and pooled around our bodies until the
sound of a snapped twig in the woods was enough to make
us shriek. The only cure was to be to be zipped in my jungle
hammock, which had screened-in sides and a canvas roof that
offered adequate protection from ravens and bats. The smell
of my father's ChapStick also helped, when he leaned in to kiss
me good night.

Even at home my parents did not call us in from the
yard until the first stars had come out. One reason for that,
I think, is because twenty-four-hour news channels had not
been invented yet. If a child got swiped from her yard or fell
down an abandoned well, people did not hear about it every
fifteen minutes until it seemed like a hundred children had
been hurt—a thousand, even—like every child in the whole
world who stayed out after dark was in imminent danger and
might never be seen again. This is not to discount the terrible
things that *do* happen to some children after dark, but simply
to note the high cost of assuming that what happened to them
will happen to all children everywhere if they are allowed to
walk in the dark.

Since religion would eventually change my attitude toward
the dark, it is worth mentioning that I received no religious
education at home. My family celebrated Christmas but not
Easter. We did not pray before meals. The same grandmother

who would later give me a .22 rifle gave me a miniature New Testament when I was ten, which was how I knew Jesus was the main character. When I flipped through the pages, he was in most of the pictures and his name was on almost every page, but that was all I knew about him, since I never read the book. At home we read *Pinocchio* instead. We read *Black Beauty, Doctor Dolittle, Little Women, The Adventures of Huckleberry Finn*. What I learned about darkness from stories, I learned from books like these—and also from the unedited works of the Brothers Grimm and Hans Christian Andersen.

According to a recent article in the *New York Times,* few parents expose their children to those works in the original these days, and some of their reasons make sense. Who wants children growing up with the idea that stepmothers are wicked, ugly people are evil, women can get by on their beauty, and princesses are all white? At the same time, I worry about children who grow up thinking that every story has a happy ending and no one gets permanently hurt along the way. In the original version of Cinderella, two pigeons peck out her nasty stepsisters' eyes, and they spend the rest of their lives as blind beggars, while Cinderella goes to live in the castle with her prince. In the original version of Snow White, the wicked Queen, who asks the huntsman to kill the young beauty and bring back her heart, ends up being forced to dance to death in red-hot iron shoes.

When three thousand British parents were polled in 2009, they listed these stories among the top ten fairy tales they no longer read to their children, along with Hansel and Gretel,

Jack and the Beanstalk, Sleeping Beauty, and Beauty and the Beast. When asked what they *did* read to their children at night, they put *The Very Hungry Caterpillar* at number one on a list that also included *Winnie the Pooh, Aliens Love Underpants,* and *What a Noisy Pinky Ponk!*[1] Since I have read only one of these, I cannot say for sure, but I am guessing that no one's eyes get pecked out in any of them.

What I learned from the original Cinderella story and others like it is that mysterious things happen in the dark. Sometimes the mystery is frightening, as when Hansel and Gretel come upon the witch's house in the woods, or when ugly Rumpelstiltskin shows up at night to save the miller's daughter by spinning straw into gold. Other times it is redeeming, as when the seven dwarves rescue Snow White from the wicked Queen's tricks, or Belle's tears fall on the Beast and turn him back into a prince. I was so sure that all these things happened in the dark that I am surprised fifty years later to discover that they did not. They did not happen in the literal dark, anyway. Instead, they happened in the dark of one child's imagination, confirming her sense that what is most true is not always evident by the bright light of day. While such stories offered me no guarantees about what kind of mysteries I might encounter in the dark, they made nighttime so much more potent than daytime that I was prepared to accept most risks.

While this brief survey does not exhaust my early lessons about darkness, it is enough to suggest that each of us has a personal history of the dark. A child who was locked in a closet as punishment will not register darkness the same way as a child who looked forward to family camping trips. A child who grew up in an urban housing project will fear things worse than coyotes when she bolts her doors at night. As universal as darkness may be, our experience of it is local. It is also social, cultural, economic, and political, since our relationship with darkness is never limited to what we have personally sensed or intuited about it. We have all been taught what to think about the dark, and most of us only have to think a minute to come up with the names of our teachers.

There are a number of children in my life whom I would do anything to protect. The problem is that they are already so well protected that they are missing out on some major life events, such as falling off horses, encountering snakes in the hayloft, and getting lost in the woods. When they come to visit me at the farm, I do what I can. I am the wicked witch who means to delay the good prince in his rush to wake them up.

The first few times my nephew Patrick came to see me, there was no competing with any of the handheld devices he brought with him. He was nine and loved all things virtual. If a horse could not fly and shoot fire from its nose, he was not interested in it. But he *was* interested in the green John Deere Gator parked by the garage, which was how I finally got him out of the house. Within the hour, this city kid was on his knees in the garden digging Gold Yukon potatoes with his bare hands—something he asked to do every time he came back after that, whether potatoes were in season or not.

Another boy, also named Patrick, drove his mother so crazy that she told him to go outside and do anything he wanted as long as she could see him from where she sat on the screen porch. Since he had red hair, he was easy to spot, but after he had picked up a few guinea hen feathers and thrown some stones, he ran out of ideas.

"Come here," I said, leading him over to a ten-pound rock next to the driveway. "Do you think you can flip that over?" He nodded. "Okay, then," I said, "but get ready to jump back, because you never know what you're going to find under a rock like that." Then I went back to the porch. Five minutes later, Patrick came to ask if I had a shoebox or jar that he could borrow. For the next hour, he turned over every rock in view of the porch, bringing his best finds inside to be viewed: baby garter snakes, bee sting scorpions, and blind translucent grubs, along with flat-headed earthworms, woolly caterpillars, and one hibernating toad. "Yes," his mother said, "that is a really great find. No, I don't want to hold it. What do you think about keeping it in your jar until you're ready to put it back?"

Last year Anna and her mother came to spend the night. I watched her being born, so she and I have known each other all her life. She can sit and listen to adults talk longer than most children can, which is why I believe she has a large interior life. She was about eight on the day that I am remembering, a blonde second-grader built like an old-fashioned wooden clothespin with straight legs and a round top. Since she lived in the city, I had planned a number of country activities for her, including one of the absolute best activities there is to do on a farm: moving young chickens from one pen to another after dark. This can be done during the daytime, but it is not pretty. If you try to catch wide-awake chickens in a pen, they will scream and fling themselves against the chicken wire like they have heard all the stories about people wringing their necks and eating them for supper. They crash into each other. They lose their feathers. They threaten to die of fright right there in front of you.

Go into the chicken house at night, however, and it is like they have had two martinis. They chuckle to each other when you come through the door, shifting around on their perches and turning their heads to one side so they can get a better look at you. If your flashlight is not too bright and you move slowly enough, you can reach right over and pick them up, tucking at least five in your apron and a couple more under one arm. The others will wait patiently right where they are until you come back for them, making as many trips as necessary to deliver all of them to their new home.

I thought Anna would enjoy this, so once the sun was down, I invited her to come with me to the chicken house. "You'll love this," I said. "Follow me." The chicken house was only about fifty yards from the house, down the hill from the garage across a patch of tall grass. The moon was so bright that night that we did not really need a flashlight, but I took one anyway, walking a couple of feet ahead of her to shine a beam in the direction we were going.

"I can't see," she complained when we turned the corner into the relative darkness beyond the garage.

"It's not far," I said, going ahead to light the way. "Your eyes will get used to it in a minute." The day had been warm, so moving through the wet grass was like walking through a sprinkler. The first fireflies were blinking in the woods, and a whole choir of cicadas was singing in the trees. "Isn't it great?" I asked, but there was no one behind me. Turning around, I scanned the grass with the flashlight, catching the gleaming eyes of dew on grass but no human ones above them. Heading back up the hill, I found Anna by following her sobs to the place where she had stopped, immobilized by fear, in the wet grass on a beautiful moonlit night.

It was not her fault. It was mine, for forgetting that she was a city girl and that walking in the dark takes some practice. But it was also the fault of everyone who taught her to fear the dark, convincing her that it is dangerous—all of it, all the time, under every circumstance—that what she cannot see will almost certainly hurt her and that the best way to protect herself from such unseen maleficence is to stay inside after dark with the doors locked and sleep with the lights on.

I do not doubt that her teachers did it because they love her. They did not want her to be kidnapped, or run over by a car, or bitten by a big dog. Forget the odds of any of these things happening for a moment. When you love a child, you do not deal in reasonable probabilities. You deal in dreadful possibilities, which spool from your mind in repeating loops like the worst stories on the news.

When you love a child, you do not even want to allow the possibility of her stepping on a piece of broken glass on the dark lawn, or twisting her ankle when she steps off a curb she cannot see, or being frightened by the sound of a screech owl. She already has enough trouble sleeping, so you wake up night after night to the sound of her whimpering and rush to persuade her that what is scaring her is only a dream.

You will do anything in your power to keep her from being afraid like that, and if night is what does it, well then, light the night. Set her in front of a television that will take her mind off the light of the moon. Buy a lamp for her room that will project stars on her ceiling. Plug night-lights into every socket between her bedroom and the bathroom. In all these ways and more, stand between her and the dark. Teach her to fear it by forbidding her to go into it by herself, accepting as collateral damage the loss of falling stars, glowworms, moonlight on spiderwebs, night owls, cicada songs, and moving chickens in the dark.

One of the books on my reading list was a collection of essays called *Let There Be Night*, including one by a Brit named James Bremner who said he was mightily afraid of the dark as a child. There was no reason for him to be afraid, he says now. He lived in a small village in western Scotland where there were no wild animals or known criminals. But there were also no streetlights or porch lights in his village, which meant that once night fell, the darkness was absolute. Every evening after supper, it was his job to take the family's empty milk bottles down to the bottom of the driveway so the milkman could swap them out next morning—a chore that put a major dent in his personal history of darkness. The driveway was only about a hundred yards long, but from the house it disappeared into complete blackness almost at once. When James finally balled up the courage to walk into it—running was not an option with glass bottles in his arms—he lived for the moment when he could set them down and race back to the house. The darkness never stopped terrifying him. Every single night it took all the courage he had.

But while his fear of the dark may have been baseless, the bravery it drew out of him stayed with him for the rest of his life. "Courage," he writes now, "which is no more than the management of fear, must be practiced. For this, children need a widespread, easily obtained, cheap, renewable source of something scary but not actually dangerous." Darkness, he says, fits that bill.[2]

As much as I love the story, it is hard to imagine it happening today. Most parents I know would give their darkness-challenged child another chore or offer to go with him. They would fit him out with a headlamp or ask the milkman to exchange the bottles on the porch instead. I also know parents who do not seem competent to decide what is scary but not actually dangerous for their children, as well as a few who embody the dangers those children most need protecting from. With all those caveats, the question remains: how do we develop the courage to walk in the dark if we are never asked to practice?

I was one of the lucky ones, at least where natural darkness was concerned. My parents did not protect me from my fear of it, but walked me into it on a regular basis, letting go of my hand for longer and longer periods of time until I grew a little bud of courage. Then they practiced letting me go alone, one of them calling out, "Have fun!" while the other called, "Be careful!" With those two good pieces of advice they helped me frame a personal history of darkness that allowed me to go places I might otherwise not have gone. Interestingly enough, they never taught me to call on God for help, perhaps because they had received so little help from that quarter themselves. It was not until I explored the God option on my own that I learned how dangerous darkness really was—not the kind under my bed or in the dark woods but the kind the Bible said was in my own heart.

The Fear of the Lord

Then the king said to the attendants, "Bind him hand and foot, and throw him into the outer darkness, where there will be weeping and gnashing of teeth."

—Matthew 22:13

My parents did not teach me to call on God for help in the dark, but neither did they teach me that darkness belonged to the devil. Unlike most of my friends, I grew up knowing nothing of Christianity except the cultural kind. My father never spoke of his Catholic childhood. When pressed, he would say only that he learned everything he needed to know about Jesus from the nuns who shamed and struck him at school until he left home at fifteen. My mother told me that when her older brother died at the age of nine, her fifty-five-year-old father drove from College Park, Georgia, to downtown Atlanta to be baptized at the Baptist Tabernacle.

"Do you know why he did that?" I asked her years later.

"I think he felt an obligation to do it for my brother," she said, "so he could believe they would be together again someday." He had already lost his first wife shortly after she gave birth to their first son, who went without oxygen for so long that he was never "quite right in the head." He waited a long time to remarry, becoming a father again in his late forties. He was fifty when my mother was born. "All I remember about the baptism is his white hair going down under the water with his white robe floating up," she said. "I was only five, so it made a big impression on me."

It made a big impression on me too, and I was not even there. If there is any such thing as Christian karma, I came into this world with plenty of it—the firstborn child of two parents with all kinds of sorrow wrapped in their earliest memories of religion. From the moment they knew I was coming, they agreed to protect me from both the sorrow and the religion.

This worked well enough until I got my driver's license. Then, during a summer honors program at a local junior college, I met an older boy named Jack. He introduced me to his sister Carol, who was in tenth grade like me. She went to a different school, but she could finish my sentences. She understood everything important about me without having to be told, including the fact that I had a serious crush on her brother. The three of us became fast friends during the summer of my sixteenth year, which was also the year that the war in Vietnam started heating up. There was no draft yet, but Jack wanted to go. The more he wanted to go, the more he wanted me to be baptized at the same church where he and Carol had accepted Jesus and turned their lives around.

I started going to church with them. Twice on Sunday and once on Wednesday night, the preacher of that church taught me things about darkness that I had never known. Without a single grinding of gears, he shifted the subject from physical darkness to spiritual darkness, using my history of the one to fuel my fear of the other. He taught me it was no mistake that "devil" and "darkness" began with the same letter, since they came from and were headed to the same place, along with Satan and all his minions. He read scripture to support his points, picking out so many verses about outer darkness, the power of darkness, and the people of darkness that bumps broke out on my arms and the back of my neck got sweaty. How had I ever been fooled into thinking darkness was enchanting? How could I have been so wrong? After I left the church on Wednesday nights, I could not get to my car fast enough, locking all the doors the minute I was safe inside. Even then it was hard to feel secure, since I had been convinced that the darkness was inside me too. Whatever courage I had developed wilted in the presence of this evil new threat.

Before too many weeks had passed, I asked to be baptized the way someone on fire asks to be hosed down. I wanted to be saved from the devouring power of darkness. I wanted Satan to know that I had gone over to the other side. The love of God had very little to do with it, though I spent a lot of time afterward trying to conjure the light of Christ inside of me so that it could fill the formerly dark cavern of sin.

I was suffering from the full solar version of Christianity, dedicated to keeping young people like me out of as many dark places as possible, including but not limited to smoky nightclubs, back alleys, dark bedrooms, shady dope dens, and dim jail cells. In many ways it was just what I needed at that point in my life. It scared me straight. It turned my face to the sun. It offered me a map with a clearly marked path on it and answered all my questions about why I should not stray from it. But it also saddled me with a kind of darkness disability that would haunt me for years to come.

Being alone outside on a dark night began to panic me in ways it never had before. Sure, everything might look beautiful on the surface—full moon, bright path, trees throwing shadows at my feet—but who knew what dark spirits were hunting those woods at night, just waiting for someone like me to come along? One evening, walking a short path between two familiar houses that I had walked all my life, I was so overcome by the fear of evil that I could feel it rising over me from behind like a wave of pure malevolence, which there was no hope of surviving without running faster than it could swell. So I ran, flinging myself through the door into the lit house like a wolf was right behind me—but since the thing that was after me had no body that could be shut out, the door offered no real relief. Spiritual darkness was like a mist that could seep under any door, rise through the cracks in any floorboards. I could not swing a stick at it or get away from it by running. My only defense was to keep the light of Christ burning brightly inside me, which meant reading the Bible, going to church, and praying every day so that the lamp of my faith did not go out.

After Jack enlisted in the army and I went off to college, Carol and I lost touch. Sunday services at my university chapel were so different from the church where I had been baptized that it was hard to believe they were the same religion. I was so relieved to find a community of faith that did not run on the fuel of fear that I became a religion major, eager to learn whatever there was to learn by the light of this kinder Christianity. But if I had hoped for a better Bible to go with it, I did not get one.

There are only about a hundred references to darkness in the Bible, but the verdict is unanimous: darkness is bad news. In the first testament, light stands for life and darkness for death. When God is angry with people, they are plunged into darkness. Locusts darken the land. People grope in the dark without light, for the day of the Lord is darkness and not light. In the second testament, light stands for knowledge and darkness for ignorance. "If thine eye be evil, thy whole body shall be full of darkness," Matthew says in the King James Version.

When the true light comes into the world, the world does not know him. Though he comes to those in darkness and the shadow of death, they love darkness more than light. On the day he dies, darkness descends on the land from noon until three. He has come as light into the world, so that everyone who believes in him shall not remain in the darkness, but some people just cannot be helped. "They are wild waves of the sea casting up the foam of their own shame," reads Jude 13; "wandering stars, for whom the deepest darkness has been reserved forever."

Yet even in the Bible, that is not the whole story about darkness. Anyone who knows the story of Abraham remembers the night God led him outside to look at the stars. The old man was deep in doubt about whether God's promise of children would ever come true. He and his wife Sarah had been waiting so long that hope was little more than a habit. All they knew was that God kept saying "soon," but soon never came. So when God said it the next time—"Do not be afraid, Abram, I am your shield; your reward shall be very great"—Abraham decided to point out the obvious.

"You have given me no offspring," Abraham said bluntly, "and so a slave born in my house is to be my heir." God did not argue with him. Instead, God told the old man to go outside and look up at the sky.

"Count the stars, if you are able," God said to Abraham, for "so shall your descendants be." It was not something that could have happened in the middle of the day. The night sky was a key player in Abraham's decision to trust God.

Later God would come to Abraham's grandson Jacob in the middle of the night, after he fled from the family he had betrayed in the worst kind of way. When Jacob could not run any longer, he lay down in the middle of nowhere and fell asleep, dreaming one of those dreams that arrives more like a vision. He saw a ladder with its feet set on the earth and its top reaching toward heaven, with the bright angels of God climbing up and down on it. That was when God said more or less the same thing to Jacob that he had said to his grandfather Abraham. "Know that I am with you and will keep you wherever you go, for I will not leave you until I have done what I have promised you." It was not something that could have happened in the middle of the day. The night vision was a key player in Jacob's decision to believe God.

Once you start noticing how many important things happen at night in the Bible, the list grows fast. Jacob wrestles an angel by a river all night long, surviving the match with a limp, a blessing, and a new name. His son Joseph dreams such dreams at night that he catches a pharaoh's attention, graduating from the dungeon to the palace to become the royal interpreter of dreams. The exodus from Egypt happens at night; God parts the Red Sea at night; manna falls from the sky in the wilderness at night—and that is just the beginning.

One of the heaviest clusters of darkness in the early books of the Bible has nothing to do with nighttime, however. It comes about three moons into the wilderness story, when the people who escaped from Egypt are camped at the foot of Mount Sinai. That is where God decided to enter into covenant with the people, the Bible says—to marry them in the full light of day with Moses as the celebrant, which means that God and Moses have some planning to do.

"I am going to come to you in a dense cloud," God says to Moses, "in order that the people may hear when I speak with you and so trust you ever after." The people will not be able to *see* God talking to Moses; they will only be able to *hear* God talking to Moses. God sets the date for three days later, but on the morning of the big day the weather seems not to be cooperating. The sky is alive with thunder and lightning. The whole top of the mountain is covered by a dark cloud, while the rest of it is shaking like a nuclear reactor about to blow. While the people watch the mountain going up in smoke, they hear a long blast from a trumpet, though no one has a trumpet. Moses seems to be in dialogue with the heavy weather, yelling into it one minute and tilting his head to listen to the thunder answer him in the next. Then God calls Moses to the top of the mountain, where God has one final instruction for him: no one down below should make any attempt to enter the dark cloud. If they do, they will die. Moses is the only one who will be allowed to survive a direct encounter with the divine.

Moses goes back down the mountain to tell the people. Then God begins to speak from the top of the mountain, the divine voice coming out of the darkness so that the people can hear actual words: "I am the LORD your God, who brought you out of the land of Egypt, out of the house of slavery; you shall have no other gods before me." That is the first clause of the covenant, with nine more behind it, rattling the people's teeth with the force of the consonants alone. When it is all over—when the people have witnessed the thunder and the lightning, when they have heard the blast of the trumpet and seen the mountain smoking—every single one of these people who have prayed and prayed to hear the voice of God does a complete about-face. "You speak to us, and we will listen," they say to Moses; "but do not let God speak to us, or we will die."

The darkness that dominates this story has nothing to do with what time of day it is. It has nothing to do with the position of the planets in the sky or the rods and cones in people's eyes. It is an entirely unnatural darkness—both dangerous and divine—that contains the presence of the God before whom there are no others. It is so different from what other Hebrew words mean when they say "dark" that it has its own word in the Bible: *araphel,* reserved for God's exclusive use. This thick darkness reveals the divine presence even while obscuring it, the same way the brightness of God's glory does. Both are signs of God's mercy, since ordinary human beings are not equipped to survive direct contact with the divine, in the dark or in the light.

This view of darkness is far more nuanced than the one that demonizes darkness. While this darkness is dangerous, it is as sure a sign of God's presence as brightness is, which makes the fear of it different from the fear of snakes and robbers. When biblical writers speak of "the fear of the Lord," this is what they mean: fear of God's pure being, so far beyond human imagining that trying to look into it would be like trying to look into the sun.

When I took my first course in Christian mysticism at the age of nineteen, I learned to call this the *mysterium tremendum et fascinans*—the terrible and fascinating mystery of God—which exceeds human ability to manage it in any way. "This darkness and cloud is always between you and God, no matter what you do," wrote the anonymous fourteenth-century author of *The Cloud of Unknowing*, "and it prevents you from seeing him clearly by the light of understanding in your reason and from experiencing him in sweetness of love in your affection. So set yourself to rest in this darkness as long as you can, always crying out after him whom you love. For if you are to experience him or to see him at all, insofar as it is possible here, it must always be in this cloud and in this darkness."[1]

A thousand years earlier, a Cappadocian monk named Gregory of Nyssa was the first to see Moses's cloud as a cipher for the spiritual life. "Moses's vision began with light," he wrote. "Afterwards God spoke to him in a cloud. But when Moses rose higher and became more perfect, he saw God in the darkness."[2] In the same way, Gregory said, those of us who wish to draw near to God should not be surprised when our vision goes cloudy, for this is a sign that we are approaching the opaque splendor of God. If we decide to keep going beyond the point where our eyes or minds are any help to us, we may finally arrive at the pinnacle of the spiritual journey toward God, which exists in complete and dazzling darkness.

What? God exists in darkness? Cloudy vision is a *good* thing? This was so different from anything I had learned in church that I had to know more—but who could teach me about this tremendous mystery? In another century I might have gone to live in a cave or a convent, but my college advisor suggested seminary instead, so that became the plan. In the fall I would become a first-year student at a reputable divinity school, but meanwhile I had three months to kill. Since waiting tables was my only marketable skill, and the best money to be made was in the high-end tourist trade, I became a cocktail waitress at Dante's Down the Hatch, a jazz club in Underground Atlanta, while I waited to go to seminary.

In most ways, this turned out to be the best preparation for a theological education that a girl could have. Every afternoon I headed into the city just as everyone else was headed out, leaving me with lots of empty parking spots from which to choose. Underground was, literally, underground—a stretch of old downtown Atlanta that was once above ground, until urban development put it in the dark by building a new roadway that raised street level one full story. The first stories of the old buildings were mothballed for years, until someone came up with the idea of turning the space into an underground playground for adult visitors to the city. By the time I got there, it looked like a leftover movie set in a Hollywood warehouse, with gas lamps lining the streets in front of the kinds of bars that serve drinks in oversize souvenir glasses.

Since Georgia summers are hot, I always looked forward to the moment of crossing the threshold between the griddle-hot parking lot and the cool cavern of Underground, where the temperature hovered around sixty degrees. On days when the humidity was high, my skin beaded up like a bottle of good Bordeaux. Even when the streets were clean, they smelled like the floors of damp caves. When the street sweepers had been through earlier in the day, small pools of water still stood in the gutters, with pigeons pecking at the popcorn kernels and bits of tobacco floating on the surface. On my short walk to work, I passed a pinball arcade, a saloon with chest-high wooden swinging doors, and a place where you could dress up like a Civil War soldier to have your picture made.

Dante's was the classiest establishment by far, an elaborate fantasy of a nightclub that featured a two-story pirate ship with a lagoon around it where live caimans lived. When I entered the club, my entrance ritual included leaning over the rail of the dock to see if I could spot one of them gliding across the mossy bottom of its faux sea. A massive stalagmite of candle wax rose from one of the pylons of the dock, the result of one votive having been placed on top of another for as long as the club had been there. Walking past it on my way to the bar, I inhaled the aroma of alcohol, candle, and reptile that meant my workday was about to begin.

Inside the ship, a jazz trio played until two o'clock most mornings while patrons consumed vast quantities of expensive liquor and ordered pot after pot of hot cheese fondue. I learned how to carry Singapore slings on a tray above my head while dodging customers on their way to and from the bathrooms, as well as how to replenish the fuel under a hot fondue pot without setting the table on fire. On a good night I made sixty dollars cash; on a great night, a hundred. The money was so compelling that I asked Dante to let me return the following summer. He was so charmed by the idea of a seminary-trained cocktail waitress that he said yes.

For the next three years, this arrangement put an interesting edge on my theological education. During the days of the school year, I took classes in ontology, ecclesiology, and eschatology, in which I was invited to order my thoughts about the nature of being human, the purpose of human community, and the future of humankind. I learned the principles of effective preaching, sound leadership, and pastoral care. On summer nights at Dante's, I dealt with businessmen who used me to prove how much power they had over people who made less money than they did, and tourists who drank so much that when I brought them their checks at the end of the night they looked at me like I was pressing a gun to their ribs. I learned that people will confess things to a stranger in a nightclub that they have never admitted to anyone they know by the clear light of day. Because I was the least significant person they knew, such people would tell me things they should have been telling a doctor, a lawyer, a psychiatrist, or a judge. I would not hear such stories again for years, until as a young priest I became a different kind of stranger to people who had no one else to tell their stories to.

Of course there were endearing customers too, like the Catholic priest who came by himself every Friday night to listen to jazz. He always wore his collar. He never ordered food, just a bottle from the high end of the wine list. As long as I kept his glass fresh for the hours he sat there, I could count on a 25 percent tip. There were also the first dates, the honeymooners, and the couples celebrating anniversaries, whose clear enjoyment of one another spilled over on everyone around them, including me.

For as long as I worked Underground, my days started after noon and ended at four in the morning, which was how I learned that a whole new world opened up after dark. The people who were awake at night were different from the people who were awake during the day. They knew things the day people did not know, like what kinds of injuries you see most often on the graveyard shift at the emergency room, or how many people leave personal items on their desks at work, forgetting that the night maintenance crew will be coming through later in the evening.

They also knew where you could get the best western omelet at three in the morning, which turned out to be the Majestic Diner on Ponce de Leon Avenue—as famous in its own way as Underground Atlanta was. After Dante's closed, those of us who were still wired from work would meet there in one of the large booths by the window, sliding across the red vinyl bench seats to take our places among all the other night workers—off-duty cops, working girls, and middle-class insomniacs, all as exotic to me as the movie stars I watched play such characters on the big screen.

What surprised me most was how much energy coursed through that place in the middle of the night, as if all the ordinary sleeping people had relinquished their portions so that there was more left for the rest of us. Sometimes, after I had taken the long way home through almost empty streets, I would stay up another couple of hours writing a short story that had begun to take shape at the Majestic Diner, fighting gravity until I fell asleep. It did not take long to become a night junkie, preferring the eccentric rhythms of the night to the comparatively dull routines of a sunny day.

All these years later, I like to think that I learned as much about human nature waiting tables at Dante's as I did writing papers for my seminary professors. One happened in the dark and one happened in the light, but together they offered me a better education in the *mysterium tremendum* than I could ever have gotten by attending just one of them. Later, when I stood in front of an altar waving incense, I would remember standing in front of the bar at Dante's waving cigarette smoke out of my face, and the exact same feeling of tenderness would wash over me, because the people in both places were so much alike. We were all seeking company, meaning, solace, self-forgetfulness. Whether we ever found those things or not, it was the seeking that led us to find each other in the cloud even when we had nothing else in common. Sometimes I wondered if it even mattered whether our communion cups were filled with consecrated wine or draft beer, as long as we bent over them long enough to recognize each other as kin.

Now, when I listen to people talk about light and darkness, it is easy to become despondent about the odds of redeeming the dark.

"That was a really dark movie," a friend says, describing a film in which the villain killed people as casually as he picked his teeth.

"I am in a dark place right now," another says while she waits for the results of a pathology report.

"Jesus is the light of the world," someone else says to her by way of consolation. "Just remember that. Even when it's so dark you can't see God, God can still see you."

I cannot remember the last time I heard anyone use "dark" to describe something good. Fear of the dark has been sanctified in so many people's minds that I have to define my terms— not once, but over and over again—because without constant reminders that darkness is not a synonym for mortal or spiritual danger, most people I know revert to the equation without even thinking about it. It is as if they have a default setting for darkness in their minds that automatically resets every time the sun comes up. In the full light of day, darkness becomes the most convenient place for them to store all their shadows: their fear of the unknown, their anxiety about the future, their loathing of their own helplessness, their bottomless dread of death.

If darkness really does bring such phantoms out of hiding, I think that is because the bright distractions of daytime have come to their natural end. When the sun goes down, it is time for another natural thing to happen, as the slower, quieter, and more tactile rhythms of nighttime open doors that remain shut during the day. No doubt there are frightening things behind some of those doors, but there are also stunning things. Eventually, with some practice, one learns that all these doors open on the same room. "I form light and create darkness," God says through the prophet Isaiah, "I make weal and create woe."

The way most people talk about darkness, you would think that it came from a whole different deity, but no. To be human is to live by sunlight and moonlight, with anxiety and delight, admitting limits and transcending them, falling down and rising up. To want a life with only half of these things in it is to want half a life, shutting the other half away where it will not interfere with one's bright fantasies of the way things ought to be.

Though my intrigue with physical darkness preceded the dread of metaphysical darkness I picked up in church, I am not insensible to the dangers of darkness. I have worked emergency rooms and county jails, slept in tents with wild things snuffling outside, and visited inmates on death row. Though I have never been the victim of a violent crime after dark, I know people who have. One bought a trained German shepherd that went everywhere with her after that. Another bought a gun. I am not sure what I would do. Although some of my experiences with darkness have been life threatening, none has involved another person who wished to do me harm.

One night on the Outer Banks of North Carolina, I walked off the end of a dock in the dark and landed thirteen feet below on a driftwood board with nails in it. Lying there waiting for my breath to come back, I remembered the yellow tape I had stepped over on my way toward the sound of the ocean—a warning that half the dock had been washed away by a hurricane earlier in the season. That was when it came to me that learning to walk in the dark might involve some actual skills and not simply bravado.

Because I live on a farm nine miles from the nearest stop-light, I also know how dangerous darkness can be for some of the creatures that live here with me. If I forget to shut the chicken house at night, there is a good chance no one will be home in the morning. One night a bunch of raccoons carried off a full dozen of my chickens, leaving a trail of feathers that led me to the carcass of a gutted rooster in the woods.

Red foxes and wild dogs will do the same thing. If chickens could buy guns, they would. But one of the scariest things that has happened to me after dark on the farm happened one night while I was collecting eggs. I knew the henhouse so well that I did not bother to take a light. I just went in, said hello to the hens, and started feeling around in their laying boxes for the day's yield.

There was a little moonlight coming in through the window, which I admired while I felt around in the first box. I found three eggs: a perfect handful. After putting them in my apron, I stuck my hand in the second box and felt something cooler than hay. Maybe it was a piece of plastic that had got-ten baled by mistake? That had happened more than once, so I kept feeling around for eggs—only there were not any, and when I touched the cool thing again it moved, uncoiling itself until I could see the head of the big black snake in silhouette, sliding noiselessly through a hole in the chicken wire.

Remembering that night now, I can dissect it better than I could then. The snake scared me, but it did not hurt me. Based

on its behavior, it was as frightened of me as I was of it. It was
not a biblical snake, come to talk me into disobeying God so
that my offspring and I would suffer from my sin forever. It
was not even a Freudian snake, come to remind me how strong
my id was. It was just a hungry black snake in search of supper,
with a brain so small that there was no room in it for any inten-
tional malice toward me. That snake's opening of its mouth for
those eggs was as natural as my jerking my hand away from its
cool body in the dark. Everything else was my invention, made
all the more vivid because I could not see.

While this darkness was only a poor cousin of *araphel*, it
alerted me to a question that would preoccupy me for months
to come: when we run from darkness, how much do we really
know about what we are running from? If we turn away from
darkness on principle, doing everything we can to avoid it
because there is simply no telling what it contains, isn't there
a chance that what we are running from is God?

Moses knew God as well as anyone ever had, yet God did
not tone anything down for him. The mountain shook like it
was about to blow apart. The cloud at the top of the mountain
was so thick that even Moses could not see inside it. Anyone
else who even tried would die, God said—and Moses went
anyway. He took the full dose of divine darkness and lived to
tell about it, though God would remain a tremendous mystery
to him for the rest of his life. After all they had been through—
the plagues, the parting of the sea, the pillars of cloud and fire
in the wilderness—God prevented Moses from entering the

land of promise. "You broke faith with me," God said at the end. "Although you may view the land from a distance, you shall not enter it."

It is hard to get from a story like that to a bumper sticker that says, "God is love." What would Moses say to people who feel free to ask God for good weekend weather and safe travel to away games? The God of Moses is not the grandfatherly type, a kind old deity who can be counted on to take the kids exciting places without letting them get hurt. The God of Moses is holy, offering no seat belts or other safety features to those who wish to climb the mountain and enter the dark cloud of divine presence. Those who go assume all risk and give up all claim to reward. Those who return say the dazzling dark inside the cloud is reward enough.

Outside my window the moon has changed shape, beginning the slow emptying that will take two full weeks to accomplish. It empties from right to left, losing light as it moves nearer the sun that will eventually make its face invisible to me. With the moon as my guide, I am on the move too, wondering about the link between inner and outer space. If outer darkness is the cloud where we store our inner fears, how much will the real world suffer from our collective fear of the dark? How much will we pay to fuel the engines that keep our world lit, rather than doing what is necessary to feel safer inside ourselves?

Hampered
by Brilliance

*We must enter into the universe of the galaxies
and the light years, even at the risk of spiritual vertigo,
and know what after all must be known.*
—Chet Raymo

Anyone in need of a tutorial on the cost of too much light does not have far to look. Every time a new gas station goes up on an old country road, the lights designed to attract sleepy motorists kill another layer of stars. Why does it matter? I can think of two reasons. First, because the Milky Way, about which Ovid wrote more than two thousand years ago, is now invisible to two-thirds of those living in the United States. If this does not bother you, that may be because you have never seen it stretched out above your head like a meadow of smallest stars. Lie down in it, even with your eyes, and you risk wondering things that will make you dizzy for days. Where does that path of stars lead? Where does the cosmos end? What lies beyond it, and who are you to wonder about such things? If you are ever in doubt about your place in the universe, this is a good way to remember.

The second reason to care about the cost of illuminating the night is because our inner and outer worlds are so closely related. For a candid photo of what is on your mind, take a look at your desk. For a measure of your comfort with the dark, notice how many lights you leave on at night. Is one per room enough or do you prefer more? Is a bright home sufficient or does the yard need to be lit too? In these ways and more, our comfort or discomfort with the outer dark is a good barometer of how we feel about the inner kind.

Several years ago, the cover of *National Geographic* featured an aerial photograph of nighttime Chicago, glittering like the lights of an oil rig on a black ocean. Actually, it glittered like the lights of a thousand oil rigs—solid acres of them, made of lights in buildings and lights on buildings, streetlights, stoplights, headlights, brake lights, elevated T lights, caution lights—lights reflected off glass, off polished stone, off water, off the surfaces of slick streets—and, if only I had been near enough to see them, off the pupils of thousands of human eyes.

The theme of the lead story was printed in big black letters that punched holes in the expanse of artificial light: "The End of Night: Why We Need Darkness." Inside was an article called "Our Vanishing Night" by Verlyn Klinkenborg,[1] a regular contributor to the op-ed page of the *New York Times*. The thesis of his article was that beauty is not the only thing night has going for it. Darkness turns out to be as essential to our physical well-being as light. We not only need plenty of darkness to sleep well; we also need it to *be* well. The circadian rhythm of waking and sleeping matches the natural cycle of day and night, which affects everything from our body chemistry to our relationships. When we tinker with it, we tinker with the well-being of every creature whose pupils shrink when we turn on the lights. What, then, shall we make of the human determination to light the night—to shrink the amount of darkness in our lives and our world to the point that all creation suffers from our inventiveness?

As anyone who ever took a biology class knows, human beings are diurnal creatures with eyes adapted to light. When we go out at night, we need light to see. Many of the creatures we glimpse in the beams of our headlights or flashlights are nocturnal creatures, with eyes adapted to darkness. They need very little light to see. For these reasons and more, it is we and not they who have bent the physical world to meet our particular needs. We are the human engineers who have filled the night with light so that our eyes work no matter what time it is.

Where I live, the worst thing a new neighbor can do is move in and install a new security light that douses the stars for the rest of us. What are they afraid of? The opossums will come up onto the porch to eat the cat food whether you leave the light on for them or not, and the deer will only be grateful to you for helping them see which of your shrubs have the most tender-looking leaves. Meanwhile, a string of security lights can suck the pleasure right out of a late-night walk in the neighborhood on a night with falling stars, the same way it ruins coming home from a long trip with too many bright lights in it.

Sometimes, when I have survived a day of three airports, two expressways, and one rush hour, turning down my dark road has resurrection in it. The deep breath comes first, opening up parts that have not had air all day. The rising feeling follows, as skin prickles with the sudden coolness coming in the windows and muscles clenched against passing trucks begin to relax. Finally an owl flies over the windshield and the soul comes out of hiding, opening in the dark like a night-blooming flower. Hello, hello, I say to the welcoming committee in the woods— all those bright eyes come to let me know that I am home.

There is a mile of this rich nightlife before I come to the driveway of the new neighbors, who have put up a security light so bright that I have to raise my hand to shield my eyes. The soul runs for cover. I am back at the airport again, back on the expressway, as suddenly furious with these people for stealing my darkness as they must be afraid of whatever this light is meant to protect them from.

It helps to remember that my fury is a luxury. If I did not have lights, I would miss them. There are so many places in the world where poverty and darkness are synonymous, where the absence of electricity means that people die sooner than they have to for all sorts of preventable reasons and rural women spend their whole lives doing things by hand that their city sisters do by flipping a switch. When the writer James Agee visited a country burial ground in Alabama during the years before rural electrification, he found women's graves decorated with dinner plates, butter dishes, and baskets made of milk glass. Others were marked with things people in those places dreamed of but never had in life. On one grave, he found a blown-out lightbulb screwed into the red clay at the exact center of it; on two or three others, insulators of blue-green glass.[2]

The brightest spots on earth have never been the places where the most people live, but rather the places where the most prosperous people live. Where there is money and power enough to light the night, darkness does not stand a chance. That is why it is so important for those of us with the resources to handle our nyctophobia, our fear of the night. The name of our dread comes from Nyx, the daughter of Chaos, one of the earliest and scariest gods of the Greeks. Her job was to ride across the sky at day's end in a chariot drawn by two pitch-black horses, drawing the curtain of night behind her as she went. The names of her children reveal their mother's character: Sleep, Death, Tribe of Dreams, Strife, Doom, and— depending on whom you ask—Eros as well.[3] Nyx conceived all those babies by herself. The only two children she had with another god were named Light and Day. Thus in Greek myth as well as in the book of Genesis, darkness precedes light.

If that list of Nyx's offspring reveals anything, it is it how long people have associated night with death and all its cousins. Even now, physicians recognize something called Sudden Unexplained Nocturnal Death Syndrome, in which death is caused by ventricular fibrillation brought on by extreme terror during one of the REM phases of sleep.[4] But most of us do not have to go that far to discover how Nyx's children got their names. All we have to do is wake up in the middle of the night and find ourselves unable to go back to sleep, so that we have several free hours to obsess about everything from how we will pay our Visa bills to who will take care of us when we can no longer take care of ourselves. Sometimes, when I wake up in the morning, I find a list by my bed that says: mammogram, cats to vet, update will, clean refrigerator, increase pension, pray more, quarterly tax, cancel Hulu. When does Nyx sleep?

There is one cure for me on nights like this. If I can summon the energy to put on my bathrobe and go outside, the night sky will heal me—not by reassuring me that I will be just fine, but by reminding me of my place in the universe. Looking up at the same stars that human beings have been looking at for millennia, I find my place near the end of the long, long line of stargazers who stood here before me. Thanks to them, I can pick out the same constellations to which they gave names: the wobbly "W" of Cassiopeia pointing to Andromeda with Pegasus above and Perseus below; the North Star in the handle of the Little Dipper pointing straight to the cup of the Big Dipper below. Long after I am gone, those stars will still be there, giving others their bearings after their beds have pitched them overboard. Then again, the stars may be gone too.

"All light is late," wrote the poet Li-Young Lee, reminding me how long it takes for starlight to reach my eyes. When I look at the stars, I may be seeing late light from some whose funerals took place a long, long time ago. Stars are light-years away; galaxies are millions of times that far away. Chet Raymo, who is to astronomy what Li-Young Lee is to poetry, tells me that if I could find Quasar 3C 273 in my backyard telescope, I would be looking at a point of light that started heading my way more than one and a half billion years ago.[5] Compared to that, the sun is a newborn. Hundreds of thousands of stars flared up and burned out again before the Milky Way galaxy delivered her first sun.

All these years later, every atom on earth comes from the sky I am looking at: hydrogen, carbon, oxygen, iron—the basic building blocks of everything from the high peaks of the Himalayas to the hollow flutes of my bones. If I cannot imagine eternal life any other way, I can start with a carbon atom, since every one that ever existed is still around here somewhere. It may have spent some time in a rock before taking up residence in the ocean, then cashed everything in for a spell in the atmosphere before moving to a plant and then a human body. Whether that body ends up in earth or fire, the carbon will go on living, joining up with a couple of oxygen atoms for one leg of the journey before taking up with some made of nitrogen or hydrogen for the next.

Every one of these atoms came to earth from the heavens. The lead in my pencil might as well declare that it is "Made in Orion" as "Made in China," Raymo says.[6] I and everything I love have come forth from the furnace of the stars by a process so full of unfathomable, life-giving grace that my earlier worrying strikes me as cheap. Having summoned the energy to put on my bathrobe and go outside, I can go back to bed now. The stars are in their heaven and all is right with the world.

If the human fear of night affected only humans, there might be justice in that. But our nyctophobia affects every creature within reach of the light we have invented to push back the dark. A few years ago, Ed and I were exploring the dunes on Cumberland Island, one of the barrier islands between the Atlantic Ocean and the mainland of south Georgia. He was looking for the fossilized teeth of long-dead sharks. I was looking for sand spurs so that I did not step on one. This meant that neither of us was looking very far past our own feet, so huge loggerhead turtle took us both by surprise.

She was still alive but just barely, her shell hot to the touch from the noonday sun. We both knew what had happened. She had come ashore during the night to lay her eggs, and when she had finished, she had looked around for the brightest horizon to lead her back to the sea. Mistaking the distant lights on the mainland for the sky reflected on the ocean, she went the wrong way. Judging by her tracks, she had dragged herself through the sand until her flippers were buried and she could go no farther. We found her where she had given up, half cooked by the sun but still able to turn one eye up to look at us when we bent over her.

I buried her in cool sand while Ed ran to the ranger station. An hour later she was on her back with tire chains around her front legs, being dragged behind a park service Jeep back toward the ocean. The dunes were so deep that her mouth filled with sand as she went. Her head bent so far underneath her that I feared her neck would break. Finally the Jeep stopped at the edge of the water. Ed and I helped the ranger unchain her and flip her back over. Then all three of us watched as she lay motionless in the surf.

Every wave brought her life back to her, washing the sand from her eyes and making her shell shine again. When a particularly large one broke over her, she lifted her head and tried her back legs. The next wave made her light enough to find a foothold, and she pushed off, back into the water that was her home. Watching her swim slowly away after her nightmare ride through the dunes, I noted that it is sometimes hard to tell whether you are being killed or saved by the hands that turn your life upside down.

"Sometimes they make it," the ranger said, "and sometimes they don't. We won't know until next year whether she was one of the lucky ones or not."

"How is that?" I asked.

"If she comes back to lay her eggs again," he said, "we'll know she survived." But who would help her next time? The lights on the mainland would still be there—even more than this year, judging from the new strip malls we had passed on our way to the ferry. When her eggs hatched, her babies would be wired to scramble toward the ocean while seabirds and ghost crabs picked off the stragglers, but the hatchlings would be subject to the same confusion as their mother. What hope did the turtles have, with their navigational system made obsolete by humans?

The same thing happens to birds. Seabirds circle the lights on marine oil platforms until they drop, while inland birds drawn by city lights become confused and collide with bright buildings. A full-page photo in the *National Geographic* article shows schoolchildren in Canada gathered around a white tarp holding more than a thousand birds from eighty-nine species collected over three months from the streets of Toronto. By my amateur count, goldfinches were the big losers by far—seven rows of crowded little yellow bodies at least—plus twenty-two purple sandpipers, fifteen red-headed woodpeckers, ten robins, seven blue jays, six flickers, three cardinals, and one lone kingfisher.

I guess it is possible to think that what is bad for these creatures remains good for us, but scientists who have studied the ill effects of light pollution on other species have begun to look into the biological effects on human beings as well. For the past two centuries, we have been performing an open-ended experiment on ourselves, some of those scientists say, though none of us signed permission slips.

Every time we turn on a light after dark, receptors in our eyes and skin send messages to our adrenal, pituitary, and pineal glands to stop what they are doing and get ready for the new day. Fluorescent lights and computer screens both flicker on and off at about 60–120 cycles a second, which is enough to fool your brain into thinking that the sun is coming up, but even the light from a cell phone charger or a glow-in-the-dark clock can cue your body that morning is under way. When that happens, your adrenal gland starts pumping more adrenaline into your bloodstream to handle the stress of an ordinary day. This tells your pituitary gland to back off on the human growth hormone your body uses to repair your muscles and bones at night. It also signals your pineal gland to stop making melatonin, the hormone that regulates your sleep, which it can only do in the dark. No wonder sleep aids have their own section in the supermarket. Turning on your bedside lamp may help you get safely to the bathroom and back, but it will also upset your chemistry.

The effects of chronic sleep deprivation include elevated blood pressure and blood glucose levels, depression of the immune system, increased risk of ulcers and heart disease, memory loss, and heightened appetite. Every nuclear accident in the world has happened on the night shift. So did the Exxon Valdez oil spill in 1989. According to the National Highway Traffic Safety Administration, driver fatigue is responsible for 100,000 accidents and 1,500 deaths every year. One study found that medical interns working through the night were twice as likely to misread hospital test results, increasing the possibility of making poor decisions for their patients.[7] The divorce rate of night workers is 10 percent higher than the national average.[8] The risk of breast cancer rises 50–70 percent for women who work night shifts.[9]

Ecological disruption, night blindness, sleep deprivation, nuclear safety, mental and physical health—all in all, we are paying a high price for our fear of the dark. Yet someone is bound to argue that without artificial light, the night would be a far more dangerous place to be—if not in the country where I live, then in cities where darkness offers cover for all kinds of people who are up to no good. I thought so too, until I read a book by Jane Brox called *Brilliant: The Evolution of Artificial Light,* in which she says that lights do not deter crime as much as their proponents hoped they would. In the 1990s, Chicago's Department of Streets and Sanitation decided to increase the lighting in the city's alleyways from 90 to 250 watts. When researchers measured the results a few months later, they found violent crime had increased by 14 percent, property crimes by 20 percent, and substance abuse violations by 51 percent. Of course there was more than one way to read those statistics. Were crimes really increasing, or did the lighting simply make it possible for more people to see and report them? Or were more people going out at night, lulled into a false sense of security by the new lights and therefore exercising less caution?

The connection between light and safety may never be fully understood, Brox says, since what light can really do and what we imagine it can do are not completely different things. If we believe a bright security light keeps us safer after dark, there is not a statistic in the world with power to persuade us otherwise. Our feelings of safety are relative, not absolute. They have everything to do with our history, our surroundings, our anxiety levels, our worldviews. The amount of light we need to feel safe is a moving target that can shift several times in a single day, depending on where we are and how we feel about it.

Given all this subjectivity, Brox says, we have good reason to wonder whether we are "hampered more by brilliance than our ancestors were by the dark."[10] Darkness is necessary to our health. Without enough of it, we make ourselves sick with light. Worse than that, we take all creation with us, making the whole planet pay for our fear of the night. After reading this, I close the book and turn off the light by my bed. It is only dark for a moment before I see the small eyes looking back at me from all over the room—phone charger, printer power button, radio dial, digital clock—plus the light on the side of my computer that tells me it is sleeping, casting a wide shadow on my wall that rises and falls with every virtual breath. How did I ever mistake this for dark?

One by one I unplug them all, though it means waking the computer up to turn it off and resetting the clock in the morning. Then I walk through the house like Nyx, drawing the curtain of darkness behind me as I go. When all the lights are off, there is still plenty of light left, both inside and outside of me. On the spot, I decide to rename my children: Rest, Hush, Tribe of Stars, Slow, Truce, and—depending on whom you ask—Dazzle. If I want to get to know them, there is no better time than now. All I have to do is sit right where I am, letting them come to me for once instead of sending them away.

The Dark Emotions

*Knowing your own darkness
is the best method for dealing with
the darknesses of other people.*

—Carl Jung

While no one's personal history of darkness is exactly like anyone else's, beds are something we all have in common. They are where most of us spend the night hours. They are where we sleep and dream. They are also where some of us wake at inconvenient hours to think about things we would rather not think about, which is why our bedside tables are littered with remedies for getting back to sleep. If the book does not work, there is solitaire. If solitaire does not work, there is the white noise machine. If the white noise machine does not work, there is a pill.

What is it about beds at night? During the daytime a bed seems harmless enough. You can take a nap in one on a Saturday afternoon without waking up wondering how much longer you have to live. You can work a crossword puzzle in one while you are getting over a bad cold without worrying about who will take care of you when you live past all sense and usefulness. But wake up in bed in the middle of the night, unable to go back to sleep, and you can be in for a real workout.

When I wake up like that, things go all right for a moment or two. The dream was just a dream. I did not really miss the only flight to France or forget to attend math class all semester. The bed is familiar. The house is quiet. Everything is all right. But then I remember that I am awake when I am supposed to be sleeping and how hard it can be to get back to sleep again, especially when I start thinking about all the things I do not want to think about, which I am beginning to think about right now. That is when I can feel the dark angel come into the room and sit down on my bed. Perhaps this is Nyx, but I do not think so. He or she, I cannot tell, but the presence feels less like the queen of the night than a heavenly chaperone come to sit with me while I visit feelings I would rather not have.

A friend of mine says he turns over and over in bed when he wakes up like this, until he has all the bedclothes wrapped around him like a bandage. One night his wife tried to get some of the covers back, yanking at them and telling him to go back to sleep.

"I can't." he whispered. "I think it's God that's bothering me."

"Well, God's not bothering me," she said, "so get up and pray, but do it somewhere else."

That is probably the best idea, but if the prayer is a plea to be returned to unconsciousness, then it is just another evasion. What if I could learn to trust my feelings instead of asking to be delivered from them? What if I could follow one of my great fears all the way to the edge of the abyss, take a breath, and keep going? Isn't there a chance of being surprised by what happens next? Better than that, what if I could learn how to stay in the present instead of letting my anxieties run on fast-forward?

By day I can outfox questions like these—racing from one appointment to the next, answering e-mails with red exclamation points by them, taking the suddenly sick dog to the vet, rummaging through the freezer for something to thaw for supper. By day, I am a servant of the urgent. Nothing important has a chance with me. I am too consumed with the things that *must* be done to consider whether or not doing them even matters. But in the middle of the night I do not have so much to do. Once the lights are off and I am lying in my bed, the dark angel knows right where to find me. I am a captive audience.

Since beds are where so many of us spend the darkest hours of the day, I decided to see what the Bible has to say about them. Aside from the Song of Solomon, where the main purpose of a bed is for making love, beds are where you commune with your own heart (Psalm 4:4), get chastened with pain (Job 33:19), meditate in the night watches (Psalm 63.6), and water your couch with tears (Psalm 6:6). A bed is where you beget children, give birth, pray, dream, weep, languish, and die. According to the Gospel of Luke, you may even get raptured there: "I tell you, on that night there will be two in one bed; one will be taken and the other left."

A bed, in short, is where you face your nearness to or farness from God. Whether you are in pain or not, whether you are an anxious person or not—even, I think, whether you are a religious person or not—a bed is where you come face-to-face with what really matters because it is too dark for most of your usual, shallowing distractions to work. You can turn on the lights if you want, but they are all artificial. The most they can do is postpone your encounter with what really matters. They cannot save you from that reckoning forever.

A few months into studying the dark, I found a book called *Healing Through the Dark Emotions* by Miriam Greenspan, a psychotherapist with thirty years' experience. Ten years into her vocation, she says, her first child, Aaron, died two months after he was born without ever leaving the hospital. Like any parent struck down by such loss, she woke up every morning in the salt sea of grief and went to bed in it every night, doing her best to keep her head above water in between. This went on for weeks, then months, during which time she could not help but notice how uncomfortable her grief was making those around her, especially when it did not dry up on schedule.

According to the *Diagnostic and Statistical Manual IV*, sometimes called "the psychiatrist's Bible," patients grieving the death of a loved one are allowed two months for symptoms such as sadness, insomnia, and loss of appetite. If their grief goes on longer than that, they may be diagnosed with depression and treated with prescription drugs. "Grief," Greenspan noticed, "perhaps the most inevitable of all human emotions, given the unalterable fact of mortality, is seen as an illness if it goes on too long."[1] Her mother, a Holocaust survivor, had actively grieved for the first ten years of Greenspan's life. "Was this too long a grief for genocide?" Greenspan wondered.

The wondering led her to explore the idea that emotions such as grief, fear, and despair have gained a reputation as "the dark emotions" not because they are noxious or abnormal but because Western culture keeps them shuttered in the dark with other shameful things like personal bankruptcy or sexual deviance. If you have ever spent time in the company of the dark emotions, you too may have received subtle messages from friends and strangers alike that you were supposed to handle them and move on sooner instead of later.

Some of us have even gotten the message that if we cannot do this on schedule, we may not have enough faith in God. If we had enough, we would be able banish the dark angels from our beds, replacing them with the light angels of belief, trust, and praise. Greenspan calls this "spiritual bypassing"—using religion to dodge the dark emotions instead of letting it lead us to embrace those dark angels as the best, most demanding spiritual teachers we may ever know.

One of the main things that tip people toward garden-variety depression, she says, is a "low tolerance for sadness." It is the *inability to bear* dark emotions that causes many of our most significant problems, in other words, and not the emotions themselves. When we cannot tolerate the dark, we try all kinds of artificial lights, including but not limited to drugs, alcohol, shopping, shallow sex, and hours in front of the television set or computer. There are no dark emotions, Greenspan says—just unskillful ways of coping with emotions we cannot bear. The emotions themselves are conduits of pure energy that want something from us: to wake us up, to tell us something we need to know, to break the ice around our hearts, to move us to act.

One December a few years back, my heart froze solid with almost no warning. I was under a big deadline at work. As the days grew shorter, I got up earlier and went to bed later, spending more and more time in the dark. Everything else got shoved to the sidelines while I made words march on pages for fourteen and fifteen hours a day. After about two weeks of this, the words told me they could not go on much longer. *Let us rest,* they begged. *Leave the house, go for a walk, call a friend, take a shower. We have to rest.*

There's no time for that, I told them. *We can't stop. We have to keep working.* Not long after that, all the words lay down and died, lying on the page like ants in a poisoned anthill: little black bodies everywhere, their legs curled up like burnt whiskers. I poked at them, but they did not move. They were truly dead and I was nowhere near finished, so I pushed them around on the page, hoping they might still be made to work. I arranged the bodies this way and that, moving whole paragraphs of stiff words from one page to another, but it was no use. There was no life left in them, and still I could not stop, because I was afraid that if I stopped I would fall into a hole I could not climb out of. What was in that hole? I did not know and did not want to know. It was dark down there, and there was no light in me. That was when I knew I was in trouble. I felt like a gravedigger who did nothing all day but dig up the bodies she had just buried so she could bury them again, since that was the only way I could think of to stay out of the hole myself.

Later, after I had met my deadline by turning in an ashcan of words smoking with despair, it was clear that something had to change. Over the next few months, I overrode all my introversion to make a life with room for more people, doing things that had seemed frivolous to me before. I made new friends, joined a yoga class in town, started every day with sitting meditation, and read historical romances at night. Gradually—so gradually that a graph of my healing would have looked like a Band-Aid from the side—the large hurt inside me shrank to a smaller one.

In Greenspan's terms, I found better ways of coping with the melancholy that was so hard for me to bear. When I stopped trying to block my sadness and let it move me instead, it led me to a bridge with people on the other side. Every one of

sadness as a bridge

them knew sorrow. Some of them even knew how to bear it as an ordinary feature of being human instead of some avoidable curse. Watching them ride the waves of their own dark emotions, I learned that sadness does not sink a person; it is the energy a person spends trying to avoid sadness that does that.

One of the best things people like me can do, Greenspan says, is to become mindful of emotions as bodily sensations. This took me back to the first time I tried to become an Episcopal priest. The process began with a yearlong program of discernment under the supervision of an elder clergyman, who assigned me and a dozen other aspirants to serve as chaplains in a variety of settings while he observed. Over the course of a year, we worked with recovering addicts, people with AIDS, and the elderly, often doing more harm than good while we did our best impersonations of ministers. At the end, we sat down in a circle to find out who was being recommended for ordination and who was not. I was not, as it turned out. Because I was not sufficiently in touch with my feelings, the supervisor said, he could not approve of my taking the next step without an additional year's work.

Within the week I was sitting at my kitchen table with a stack of white copy paper on one side and a box of colored pencils on the other, intent on getting in touch with my feelings. First I drew the silhouette of a human body on a blank piece of paper. Then I wrote RAGE at the bottom. Okay, so how did rage feel? I used the black pencil to draw a storm of buzzing bees around my head, filling them with yellow. After that I made my head red: hot, hot, hot. Then I filled the whole top part of my torso with a brown tangle of electrical wires shooting sparks. Yes, I thought, holding the page out so I could see it all, that was pretty much how rage felt.

Next I did MISERY, but as soon as I wrote the word on the page, I knew it should be SAD. That called for lots of purple tears in my chest, plus a compression of the shoulders so that they sagged toward the ground. Then I used a gray pencil to put a dense little radioactive pellet of sorrow right in the middle of my body and to fill my feet with lead. That left a lot of the body still empty, so I let myself feel sad again and knew what was missing. Sadness happens in the heart. It rolls around in there and makes a lot more room, even if the stretching hurts. So I drew a large red heart on top of the purple tears and the gray pellet, making them look small by comparison. Then I used the purple pencil to sign the drawing "Sad Barbara."

After I had worked my way through most of the dark emotions, I decided to try JOY. That word called for a bright yellow ball in the middle of my chest with golden shafts of light radiating out in every direction. I used the same pencil to draw golden beams of light shooting out of my fingers, filling in the page with solid green earth under my feet and deep blue sky around my head. Then I gave myself some company, drawing lots of little stick people standing between the earth and the sky with me, all radiating the same light so that the halos of our bodies all ran together.

This went on and on, until most of the paper was gone and my refrigerator was covered with drawings that looked like the work of a second grader. Examining my night's work, the first thing I could see was that feelings do not happen only in the brain. They happen in the feet, the hands, the shoulders, and the skin, kicking up sparks in the dark interior of the body before they ever make it to the resolution center in the brain.

The second thing I could see was that I had segregated my feelings without even thinking about it, putting all of the "dark" ones on one side and all of the "light" ones on the other.

Who had taught me to do that? The sorting was so automatic that it had not required any conscious effort at all. Was it simply the difference between pleasant and unpleasant emotions or was there more to it than that?

Clearly, all the drawings were true, which made them all valuable in some way or another. Sadness went to parts of my body that Joy did not touch. Rage had the most horsepower by far, but only until it ran into Hurt. Then those two fell into each other's arms and cried until Relief covered them both. Even though I had drawn the emotions on different pages, there was no keeping them apart. The only real difference between Anxiety and Excitement was my willingness to let go of Fear. Sometimes, when I was anxious, all I had to do was take a deep breath, and my nervousness turned to anticipation.

Embarrassment and Daring were also close together. When I tried new things, I often failed at first, which was where the embarrassment came in. But if I could get over my fear of failure, there was really nothing in my way. I could be as daring as I dared to be. Every day, all these emotions gave rise to one another, overpowered one another, tempered and transformed one another in ways that never worked the same way twice. Labeling some of them "dark" all of a sudden struck me as superstitious, a reinforced ritual of disapproval designed to push away the less pleasant emotions.

When I became a hospital chaplain less than a year later, I no longer needed the drawings to remind me of how my feelings felt. My bed was a busy place back then, at least when I was on call. I might get a couple of hours of sleep before my beeper went off and I was called to the emergency room, the neonatal intensive care unit, or the psych ward, where someone was asking for a chaplain. The light in those hospital corridors was sickening at night: fluorescent and faintly green, with the occasional dying bulb buzzing and popping overhead as I made my way to whatever crisis awaited. One of the hardest things I learned to tolerate that year was the contrast between the quiet, solitary walk to my destination—with just one set of footsteps echoing down the hallway—and the noisy, roiling emotion that usually hit me as soon as I walked into a hospital room.

I still remember the woman who wailed and fell to the floor when she saw me. She knew her husband was dead, but when she saw me with a Bible instead of a stethoscope, the finality hit her like a fireball. Once she went down, her whole family started wailing too. My heart hit the gas pedal. FEAR: draw a big drum in the chest where the heart should be. Put lots of sound waves around it that extend beyond the body, since anyone within three feet can hear the chaplain's heart pounding. Then draw hairs standing up on the neck and the arms, most visibly on the arm being outstretched to shake hands with the woman's son.

"I am the chaplain on call. What can I do?" Put that in a balloon over the head. Make sure the whites of the eyes show. Then take down Fear and put up Sorrow, as the chaplain and the son help the woman up off the floor, and a long night of singing spirituals and telling stories about the life of the man who has just died begins.

Nights like that taught me the importance of letting emotions flow—even the loud and messy ones—because if they are kept from making their noise and maybe even tossing the furniture, they can harden like plaque in a coronary artery, blocking anything else that tries to come through. Eruptions are good news, the signal that darkness will not stay buried. If you can stand the upsetting energy, you may be allowed to watch while dark and light come back into balance.

Most nights I got to watch this happen more than once. After folding up the sofa bed and washing my face with a faded bar of hospital soap, I would show up at morning report looking like one of the undead, eager to hand off the beeper to whoever got it next. Yet I remember that year as one of the richest I ever spent. Every morning I knew I would be asked to do things that mattered. Every night I thought of things I could have done better but never doubted that they were worth doing. The dreams were awful—lots of IV tubes, bloody urine bags, and gray bodies on steel gurneys—but since even those knit me to people I cared about, I let them in. Feeling those splinters of other people's pain seemed like the least I could do, if only in my dreams.

Greenspan says that painful emotions are like the Zen teacher who whacks his students with a flat board right between their shoulder blades when he sees them going to sleep during meditation. If we can learn to tolerate the whack—better yet, to let it wake us up—we may discover the power hidden in the heart of the pain. Though this teaching is central to several of the world's great religions, it will never have broad appeal, since almost no one wants to go there. Who would stick around to wrestle a dark angel all night long if there were any chance of escape? The only answer I can think of is this: someone in deep need of blessing; someone willing to limp forever for the blessing that follows the wound.

What such people stand to discover, Greenspan says, is the close relationship between "individual heartbreak and the brokenheartedness of the world."[2] While those who are frightened by the primal energy of dark emotions try to avoid them, becoming more and more cut off from the world at large, those who are willing to wrestle with angels break out of their isolation by dirtying their hands with the emotions that rattle them most.

In this view, the best thing to do when fear has a neck hold on you is to befriend someone who lives in real and constant fear. The best thing to do when you are flattened by despair is to spend time in a community where despair is daily bread. The best thing to do when sadness has your arms twisted behind your back is to sit down with the saddest child you know and say, "Tell me about it. I have all day." The hardest part about doing any of these things is to do them without insisting that your new teachers make you feel better by acting more cheerful when you are around. After years of being taught that the way to deal with painful emotions is to get rid of them, it can take a lot of reschooling to learn to sit with them instead, finding out from those who feel them what they have learned by sleeping in the wilderness that those who sleep in comfortable houses may never know.

"One does not become enlightened by imagining figures of light," Carl Jung wrote, "but by making the darkness conscious."[3] Reading this, I realize that in a whole lifetime spent with seekers of enlightenment, I have never once heard anyone speak in hushed tones about the value of *endarkenment*. The great mystics of the Christian tradition all describe it as part of the journey into God, but it has been a long time since *The Cloud of Unknowing* was on anyone's bestseller list. Today's seekers seem more interested in getting God to turn the lights *on* than in allowing God to turn them *off*. Full solar spirituality strikes again.

Ken Wilber is not a Christian mystic. He has so many degrees and has written on so many subjects that most people simply call him an integral thinker who has been influenced by Eastern philosophy, but he understands how religious faith works as well as anyone I know. In a book called *One Taste,* he makes a distinction between two important functions of religion. The first function, which he calls *translation,* offers people a new way of translating the world around them so that their lives take on more meaning.

One function of Christian faith, for instance, is to offer believers a new way to translate their hardships. "Blessed are the poor in spirit," Jesus says in the Sermon on the Mount, "for theirs is the kingdom of heaven. Blessed are those who mourn, for they will be comforted." In these beatitudes, spiritual poverty and grief are moved from the "loss" side of the ledger to the "gain" side, enabling those who suffer to view their hardships as blessings. This is the function of religion that sells books and grows churches, Wilber says, because it strengthens the believer's sense of self, holding out the promise of contentment to anyone who can live by this new translation. In this mode, religion offers hope that the self may be saved.

But translation is not the only function of religion. The second function, which Wilber calls *transformation,* exists not to comfort the self but to dismantle it. "Those who find their life will lose it," Jesus says later in Matthew's Gospel, "and those who lose their life for my sake will find it." The Greek word for "life" in this passage is *psyche:* the human breath, life, or soul. While Greek has no word for "ego" (a word that did not exist in any language before the early nineteenth century), *psyche* comes close. The salvation of the *psyche* begins with its own demise.

This function of religion does not sell well, Wilber says, because it does not locate the human problem in the spiritual shortfall of the world. It locates the problem in the spiritual grasping of the self, which is always looking for ways to improve its own position. In popular American usage, Wilber says, "soul" has come to mean little more than "the ego in drag," and much of what passes for spiritual teaching in this country is about consoling the self, not losing it. Translation is being marketed as transformation, which is why those who try to live on the spiritual equivalent of fast food have to keep going back for more and more. There is no filling a hole that was never designed to be filled, but only to be entered into. Where real transformation is concerned, Wilber says, "the self is not made content; the self is made toast."[4]

If this is endarkenment, no wonder the line of seekers is so short. Even the crowds around Jesus vanished once it became clear where he was headed. He had twelve disciples the night he was arrested; three days later, only one was left, having promised Jesus he would take Mary home once there was nothing she or anyone else could do. Where did the others go? To find new lives with someone who did not ask so much of them, or at least to save the lives they still had.

As much as I do not want to go there, there is no dodging the next cycle of the moon. Above my head, the waning crescent is headed toward full dark, or at least dark to me. Paradoxically, the nights when the old moon vanishes from sight are the same nights the new moon is being born.

Tomorrow night I will need a flashlight to shut the chickens in for the night—either that, or leave the house early enough to wait for my eyes to adjust, allow for stillness, and then see what is possible. To walk like that is to become part of the night in a way that no light-bearing colonist can. To walk like that is to remember the night inside me, where the new moon is always being fashioned in the dark.

Making Toast { Appliances

The Eyes
of the Blind

To know the dark, go dark. Go without sight,
and find that the dark, too, blooms and sings.
—Wendell Berry

There are so many darknesses I will never know. The more I talk to other people about their experience of the dark, the more they remind me how personal it is. Someone with dark skin tells me what it is like to live among people who do not think twice about using "dark" as shorthand for sinister, sinful, tragic, or foul. Someone from northern Canada tells me how precious darkness is in midsummer, when the sun does not go down until midnight and is back in the sky by five. Most arrestingly of all, someone holding the harness of a seeing-eye dog asks me if I know what "darkness" means to someone who is blind.

No, I do not. Any sighted person who knows the story of Helen Keller has probably wondered about that. What does "blue" mean to someone who is blind, or "dawn," or "What you're looking for is right over *there*"? I do know how often scripture equates blindness with spiritual failure. When Jeremiah cannot get the foolish people of Judah to listen to him, he says that they have eyes but do not see. When Jesus berates the Pharisees for leading people astray, he calls them blind guides. Even now, when we criticize others for being aimless or idle, we say that they are shortsighted or have no vision.

If the metaphors work, it is because those of us who *can* see rely so heavily on our sight.

By most estimates, 70 percent of our sense receptors are located in our eyes. When they are working, they can take over most of the duties of all other senses.[1] On a night with no moon, it is not only possible to see the distant glow of the nearest town on the horizon; if you lived on a prairie with no trees, you could also see a single candle in a window ten miles away. Astronauts can see the rainforests of Brazil burning from outer space. They can find Paris by the brightness of its lights. There is so much more visual information available to most of us than we really want to see that we close our eyes to think, to kiss, or to listen.

Vision requires very little intimacy. In the age of radio waves and fiber optics, sound does not require much more.

Thanks to Skype, I can see and hear someone halfway around the world if I want to, though a handwritten letter with a foreign stamp still means more. Sight and sound both come at me with such velocity every day that I have learned to defend myself against them. If I do not limit their access to me, I will grow such thick calluses that I am no longer capable of seeing or hearing things that really matter.

My three remaining senses are in less danger, since they require greater closeness. Smell still works at some distance, though the smells that affect me most are those I pick up at short range, like the smell of the hollow at the base of my husband's neck. In order to touch that hollow, I must be within arm's reach of it. To taste it, even closer. After dark, when my eyes have semiretired for the night, all these other senses wake up. With the day's barrage of sights and sounds toned down, it is possible to savor things that slip right past me in the light. Food tastes better by candlelight. Conversations last longer. The smell of the vineyard is in the wine.

This is the basic idea behind the Blindekuh restaurant in Zurich, opened by four blind entrepreneurs in the late 1990s, where diners still make reservations months ahead to eat in the dark. A German word that translates as "blind cow," *blindekuh* is the name for the child's game of Blind Man's Bluff. The restaurant's owners were inspired by a blind Swiss pastor named Jürg Spielmann who routinely blindfolded the dinner guests who came to his house. He said they paid more attention to the food that way, and they also listened to each other better.[2]

The idea apparently caught on, since it is now possible to dine in the dark in Paris, Montreal, and Tel Aviv. I also found listings for the Opaque restaurant group in San Francisco, Los Angeles, Dallas, and New York. The basic routine in all these places is the same. First diners are taken to a softly lit lounge where they check their belongings and place their orders from a prix fixe menu. Then a blind host guides them to their seats in the pitch-black dining room, where they can hear all the usual sounds of a busy restaurant without seeing who is making any of them. In Zurich, waiters wear jingle bells on their shoes. In Paris, every dropped fork is met with waves of laughter. Patrons learn to pour their own wine by slipping one finger inside their wine glasses and tipping the bottle until they can feel wine on their fingertip. Their server teaches them to receive their dishes at the corners of their tables and to pass them to one another at the same point. Once their plates are in front of them, the server coaches them on where to find their food. *Grilled salmon at twelve o'clock, sir, roasted potatoes at nine, and snap peas at three.*

Most diners post positive reviews, offering practical advice for those who will follow. Several suggest visiting the restroom to wash your hands before being seated, since you are bound to abandon your silverware after the first course. Others advise wearing black if you are going anywhere else afterward. Nick K. offered another solution. "When the first course came out, I took my shirt off," he wrote. "I mean, why not? No one could see me. I considered taking off my pants too, but I worried I would lose them in the dark. Regardless, I ate without a shirt for the entire meal. It felt good."[3]

One of the most surprising things is how many people decide to keep their eyes closed during dinner. Anissa H., who went to Opaque for her birthday, received a long-stemmed red rose and a birthday card in Braille. It was an experience like no other, she wrote, but "the funny thing is, the whole time I had my eyes closed because it actually felt more comfortable than keeping them open. Having my eyes open and seeing nothing but pitch darkness and stars because my eyes were working overload trying to focus felt so unnatural."[4]

Reading that made me remember a chapter from Annie Dillard's book *Pilgrim at Tinker Creek*, in which she tells the story of a young woman who dealt with her sight-restoring surgery by walking around the house with her eyes closed. Like others before her, she was apparently overwhelmed by the tremendous size of the world, which she had previously measured by touch. She may also have been distressed to realize that she had been visible to other people all along—sometimes unattractively so—without her knowledge or consent. Whatever it was, her father reported that she was never happier or more at ease than when, by closing her eyes, she returned to her former state of total blindness.[5]

When I heard about an exhibit in Atlanta called "Dialogue in the Dark," the needle on my darkness meter bent toward the red zone. What dialogue, with whom, in what kind of dark? It turned out to be the Atlanta version of an installation that had toured 150 cities in more than thirty countries since its inception in the late 1980s—the brainchild of a German social entrepreneur named Andreas Heinecke. When Heinecke agreed to design a rehabilitation program for a newly blind colleague, he not only gained new understanding of the practical difficulties faced every day by those who are blind; he also noticed how sighted people treated them—with everything from pity and fear to subtle contempt.

Guided by a quotation from the Jewish German philosopher Martin Buber—"The only way to learn is through encounter"—Heinecke decided to create a physical experience of darkness that would allow sighted and blind people to change places. Dialogue in the Dark was the result—a kind of reality show in which sighted people are given red-tipped white canes before entering a completely dark exhibition hall where they are introduced to their blind guides.[6]

I purchased my tickets on a website with the headline "Where the Blind Really Do Lead the Blind," recruiting two friends to go with me so I would have someone to compare notes with afterward. When we arrived early on the appointed night, the sighted person at reception directed us to a bank of lockers against one wall and told us to leave our valuables there. "Also your watch, your cell phone, and anything else that gives off light," she said. "Might as well leave your glasses too, since you won't be needing them."

This felt so much like getting ready for a medical procedure that my heart went wobbly inside my chest. After I had put everything but my clothes in the locker, I joined my friends at the door of the exhibit, where we made lame jokes along with everyone else in our small group. The receptionist pointed to an umbrella stand near the door that was full of white canes. "Choose one that's the right height," she said. The jokes stopped after that. Most of us had seen people making their way down sidewalks with such sticks. "We" were about to become "them." Soon after, the door opened and a recorded voice instructed us to enter and sit down on one of the wooden cubes we would find inside.

The small anteroom was softly lit, so the seats were still visible. "Starting now," the voice said while the light dimmed, "notice how much you rely on sight in the course of an ordinary day. Notice how much this costs you in terms of your other senses, which you are about to use as you may never have used them before. Do what your guide tells you. If you need help, do not be afraid to ask for it. Enjoy your dialogue in the dark."

At least I think that is what the voice said. By that time, I was so busy noticing how dark it was that I was not listening very well. Was that a man or a woman who had been sitting across from me? I could hear both voices in the room but not where they were coming from. A slight breeze stirred as a new voice spoke into the dark. "Hello," a woman said. "My name is Dolores and I am legally blind, but tonight I am your best bet of getting from one end of this exhibit to the other, so why don't you stand up and follow me into the first gallery? Just follow the sound of my voice, and don't forget your canes."

For the next hour, I did my best to follow Dolores's voice, though this did not prevent me from running into walls, missing doorways, stepping on other people's heels, and tripping over my own cane. The first space we walked into was full of bird sounds. "Enjoy the park," Dolores said. "There's a bridge over a stream and a nice grassy spot on the other side, but don't dawdle. We have a lot to do." I found the handrail of the bridge without too much trouble and listened to the water flowing underneath me. Then I missed the step down at the end and landed hard against the back of the person in front of me.

He was definitely a he—taller than I—and his shirt smelled clean, though for once I had nothing more to go on. I did not know if he was old or young, white or black, pleasant to look at or not. There was no body language for me to read, no visual data to help me form judgments about who he was or what he was like. This was unexpectedly refreshing, like being at a party when the lights go out. The normal rules of polite social interaction were suspended. Furthermore, he could not see me any better than I could see him, which meant that I was excused from his judgments of me as well.

The next room was a grocery store. "Go ahead and feel what is on those shelves and in those coolers," Dolores said. "There's produce in the bins behind you too." When I found things about which there was no doubt, like a bunch of grapes or a head of cabbage, my fingers lit up. *See?* they said to my eyes. *We can do this without your help.* Canned goods were another thing altogether. Without sight, the difference between sixteen ounces of peas and sixteen ounces of Chef Boyardee was completely beyond me. The store was small, but I still got turned around in it, so Dolores's voice came from behind me when it was time to go.

"This way to the street," she said.

"Which way?" I asked.

"Walk toward my voice," she said. When I did, I found the double glass doors of the store and pushed through them to land on a sidewalk outside. Confronted with the sound of traffic for the first time, I forgot everything I ever knew about respecting other people's personal space. So did everyone else. We huddled together, unsure whether the horns were honking at us because we were standing in the street or because our light had turned green and we could not see it.

"When you hear the pedestrian signal beep, that means it is safe to cross the street," Dolores said, but the information was hard to trust. The signal meant cars were *supposed* to stop, not that they *would* stop. It did not know who was driving while texting, eating a leaky hamburger, or edging forward to make a right turn on red without checking the crosswalk first. Was anyone really looking out for me when I could not look out for myself?

As I stood rooted to the sidewalk, the voices of the others grew fainter and fainter. No one called out or came back to get me. As often as I had heard the biblical story about the one stray sheep in the wilderness, I had always assumed that the sheep was to blame for wandering away from the flock in search of better clover. But I had not moved. My shepherd had told me to walk toward her voice, but fear had prevented me. Now all of a sudden I was more afraid of being left behind than of being run over.

I stepped into the street. A horn blared. I waved my cane wildly in the air. When it made no contact, I remembered that the cars were not real, but that did not stop me from shaking like a cat in a thunderstorm. When I stumbled over the curb, I bumped into another member of the group, who was as surprised by me as I was by her.

"I don't know where they went," she said, "so I thought I'd just stand here until someone came back for me." Made brave by one another's company, we felt our way along the walls until we entered a new room full of voices. "The boat will be here any minute," Dolores said. "Just watch your step when you walk down the ramp." I had lost my friends. I was tired of feeling incompetent. When my turn came, I dropped into the boat, ready for my dialogue with the dark to be over. But I was also aware of how blindness had split the distance between me and all these other people. Touching was inevitable; apologies were redundant. We were not embarrassed to be dependent on each other. Since none of us could be sure who was black or white, young or old, our exchanges were free of any ideas we had about those identity markers. Maybe someone should start an Opaque Church, where we could learn to give up one kind of vision in hope of another. Instead of wearing name tags, we would touch each other's faces. Instead of looking around to see who's there, we could learn to listen for each other's voices.

In the last room, Dolores invited us to take a seat at the bar and order a drink from the bartender if we wanted one. Since soft drinks were the only kind on offer, I passed, half listening as Dolores thanked us for visiting the exhibit. Then someone pushed open a door and we all walked blinking into the light of the lobby.

It was like seeing people you had slept next to in a gym during a power outage—people who knew that you snored or talked in your sleep without knowing anything else about you. Appearances restored, we all stole looks at one another as we parked our canes and retrieved our belongings from our lockers, offering quick little waves good-bye without meeting each other's eyes. As I was strapping my watch back on my wrist, I looked up to see an African American woman with milky eyes come through the same door I had just exited, sweeping her cane in front of her.

"Good-night, Dolores," the receptionist said.

"See you tomorrow," Dolores said, as I watched my blind guide walk into the night.

I still do not know what darkness means to someone who is blind, but I am beginning to understand that "light" has as many meanings as "dark." There is an old prayer in *The Book of Common Prayer* that goes like this:

Look down, O Lord, from your heavenly throne, and illumine this night with your celestial brightness; that by night as by day your people may glorify your holy Name; through Jesus Christ our Lord. Amen.[7]

Among other things, this prayer recognizes a kind of light that transcends both wave and particle. It can illumine the night without turning on the lights, becoming apparent to those who have learned to rely on senses other than sight to show them what is real. This is the light the mystics see when they meditate in the night hours, picking up their pens in the morning to write down their revelations. It is the light Moses saw in the darkness on Mount Sinai, where the glory of God came wrapped in dazzling darkness. Dionysius the Areopagite called it "the unapproachable light in which God dwells."

My guess is that this idea is as incomprehensible to those who have not experienced it as it is indisputable to those who have. No one has described it better for me than Jacques Lusseyran, a blind French resistance fighter who wrote about his experience in a memoir called *And There Was Light*. Lusseyran was not born blind, though his parents noticed he was having trouble reading and fitted him with glasses while he was still quite young. Beyond that, he was an ordinary boy who did all the things that other boys do, including getting into fights at school. During one such scuffle, he fell hard against the corner of his teacher's desk, driving one arm of his glasses deep into his right eye while another part of the frame tore the retina in his left. When he woke up in the hospital, he could no longer see. His right eye was gone, and the left was beyond repair. At the age of seven, he was completely and permanently blind.

As he wrote in a second volume, he learned from the reactions of those around him what a total disaster this was. In those days, blind people were swept to the margins of society, where those who could not learn how to cane chairs or play an instrument for religious services often became beggars. Lusseyran's doctors suggested sending him to a residential school for the blind in Paris. His parents refused, wanting their son to stay in the local public school, where he could learn to function in the seeing world. His mother learned Braille with him. He learned to use a Braille typewriter. The principal of his school ordered a special desk for him that was large enough to hold his extra equipment. But the best thing his parents did for him was never to pity him. They never described him as "unfortunate." They were not among those who spoke of the "night" into which his blindness had pushed him. Soon after his accident, his father, who deeply understood the spiritual life, said, "Always tell us when you discover something."[8]

In this way, Lusseyran learned that he was not a poor blind boy but the discoverer of a new world, in which the light outside of him moved inside to show him things he might never have found any other way. Barely ten days after his accident he made a discovery that entranced him for the rest of his life. "The only way I can describe that experience is in clear and direct words," he wrote. "I had completely lost the sight of my eyes; I could not see the light of the world anymore. Yet the light was still there."

Its source was not obliterated. I felt it gushing forth every moment and brimming over; I felt how it wanted to spread out over the world. I had only to receive it. It was unavoidably there. It was all there, and I found again its movements and shades, that is, its colors, which I had loved so passionately a few weeks before.

This was something entirely new, you understand, all the more so since it contradicted everything that those who have eyes believe. The source of light is not in the outer world. We believe that it is only because of a common delusion. The light dwells where life also dwells: within ourselves.[9]

At first I thought he was speaking metaphorically—or perhaps theologically—but as I continued to read, it became clear that he was also speaking literally of an experience of light that had nothing to do with his eyes. With practice, he learned to attend so carefully to the world around him that he confounded his friends by describing things he could not see. He could tell trees apart by the sounds of their shadows. He could tell how tall or wide a wall was by the pressure it exerted on his body.

"The oak, the poplar, the nut tree have their own specific levels of sound," he wrote by way of explanation. "The tone of a plane tree is entered like a room. It indicates a certain order in space, zones of tension, and zones of free passage. The same is true of a wall or a whole landscape."[10] If Lusseyran had not already established himself as a trustworthy guide, that might have sounded crazy to me, but since he had won my confidence, I was persuaded that I was the one who was handicapped, not he.

Why had I never paid attention to the sounds of trees before? Surely the leaves of an oak made a different sound in the wind than the needles of a pine, the same way they made a different sound underfoot. I just never bothered to listen, since I could tell the trees apart by looking. When a sighted friend told me that she had been to a workshop where she learned how to listen to trees, I was taken aback.

"What do they *say*?" I asked incredulously.

"You don't want to know," she replied ruefully. Acid rain, pine beetles, clear-cutting developers—what did I *think* trees talked about?

The problem with seeing the regular way, Lusseyran wrote, is that sight naturally prefers outer appearances. It attends to the surface of things, which makes it an essentially superficial sense. We let our eyes skid over trees, furniture, traffic, faces, too often mistaking sight for perception—which is easy to do, when our eyes work so well to help us orient ourselves in space.

Speed is another problem. Our eyes glide so quickly over things that we do not properly attend to them. Fingers do not glide, Lusseyran points out. To feel a table is a much more intimate activity than seeing it. Run your hands across the top and you can find the slight dip in the middle of the center panel that you might otherwise have missed, proof that this table was planed by hand. After that, your fingers work in inches instead of feet, counting the panels by finding the cracks that separate them, locating the burn—sickle-shaped, like the bottom edge of a hot skillet—and a large burl as well. You can smell the candle wax before you find it, noting the dents left here and there by diners who brought their silverware down too hard.

By the time you reach the legs, you know things about this table that someone who merely glances at it will never know. You know that a patch on one of the legs came unglued and fell off sometime during the past century, and that someone raised the overall height of the table by adding globes below each foot. Until very recently, I would have said that the one thing you cannot tell without looking is what kind of wood the table is made of, but that was before I visited the violin maker who taught me about the sounds of different woods. He used only spruce for the front, he said, and maple for the back. Then he picked up a rough cut of each and rapped them with his knuckles so even I could hear the difference. If the violin maker were blind, I think he could have figured out that the table was made of walnut, heavy and dense from years of slow growth.

If this does not sound particularly spiritual to you, that may have more to do with you than with the table. Every major spiritual tradition in the world has something significant to say about the importance of paying attention. "Look at the birds of the air," Jesus said. "Consider the lilies of the field." If you do not have the time to pay attention to an ordinary table, how will you ever find the time to pay attention to the Spirit?

"Since becoming blind, I have paid more attention to a thousand things," Lusseyran wrote.[11] One of his greatest discoveries was how the light he saw changed with his inner condition. When he was sad or afraid, the light decreased at once. Sometimes it went out altogether, leaving him deeply and truly blind. When he was joyful and attentive, it returned as strong as ever. He learned very quickly that the best way to see the inner light and remain in its presence was to love.

In January 1944, the Nazis captured Lusseyran and shipped him to Buchenwald along with two thousand of his countrymen. Yet even there he learned how hate worked against him, not only darkening his world but making it smaller as well. When he let himself become consumed with anger, he started running into things, slamming into walls, and tripping over furniture. When he called himself back to attention, the space both inside and outside of him opened up so that he found his way and moved with ease again. The most valuable thing he learned was that no one could turn out the light inside him without his consent. Even when he lost track of it for a while, he knew where he could find it again.

If we could learn to be attentive every moment of our lives, he said, we would discover the world anew. We would discover that the world is completely different from what we had believed it to be. Because blindness taught him that, he listened with disbelief as the most earnest people he knew spoke about the terrible "night" into which his blindness had pushed him. "The seeing do not believe in the blind," he concluded, which may help explain why there are so many stories in the Bible about blind people begging to be healed. Whoever wrote down those stories could see.

In seminary I was taught to interpret them as teachings about *spiritual* blindness, but no matter how you read them, it is clear that Jesus heals only a very small percentage of those who ask for his help. There is also that strange thing he says at the end of a long healing story in John's Gospel. "I came into this world for judgment," he says after healing a man who has been blind from birth, "so that those who do not see may see, and those who do see may become blind."[12]

Before reading Lusseyran, I always heard that as a threatening judgment. Now it sounds more promising to me. At the very least, it makes me wonder how seeing has made me blind—by giving me cheap confidence that one quick glance at things can tell me what they are, by distracting me from learning how the light inside me works, by fooling me into thinking I have a clear view of how things really are, of where the road leads, of who can see rightly and who cannot. I am not asking to become blind, but I have become a believer. There is a light that shines in the darkness, which is only visible there.

Tonight there will be no moon in the sky. For close to three days it will rise and set with the sun, leaving the stars alone to light the night. I always wondered why it took "three days" for significant things to happen in the Bible—Jonah spent three days in the belly of the whale, Jesus spent three days in the tomb, Paul spent three days blind in Damascus—and now I know. From earliest times, people learned that was how long they had to wait in the dark before the sliver of the new moon appeared in the sky. For three days every month, they practiced resurrection.

"Amazing grace, how sweet the sound, that saved a wretch like me. I once was lost but now am found, was blind but now I see." Maybe. Maybe that is how grace works, but tonight it seems equally possible that the grace I need will come to me in the dark, where I too may learn to see the celestial brightness that has nothing to do with sight.

Entering
the Stone

In a dark time,
the eye begins to see.
—Theodore Roethke

Midway through my study of darkness, a new friend offered to take me into a cave.

The only caves I had ever been in were "show caves," rigged out with handrails and colored lights for the pleasure of paying customers. When I was young and family vacations consisted of road trips with my father at the wheel, there was no passing one of these without going in. Since all my sisters and I wanted to do was read comic books in the backseat of the car, we began pleading the moment a billboard or lettered barn roof came into view. It did not matter whether the sign said "See Rock City" or "Mammoth Cave." We did not want to go. Caves were dark and wet and all alike. They smelled like the insides of trash cans. The handrails were sticky, and the paths were too narrow. When you had seen one, you had seen them all.

But the man who offered to take me caving did not have a show cave in mind. His name was Rockwell. He was a retired Presbyterian minister who had been exploring caves for more than fifty years. He and his wife, Marrion, owned a home in West Virginia near one of the largest cave complexes in the United States. When he heard that I was writing a book on darkness, he asked if I would like to experience the total darkness inside a "wild" cave. The idea scared me, which made it a good opportunity to practice courage. Plus, I knew that the Buddha, Jesus, and Muhammad had all spent significant time in caves, along with Saint Patrick and Saint Francis. What drew them to those dark places, which others worked so hard to stay out of, and what did they find there that made them go back? Yes, I said, I would like to go into a wild cave.

On a cool day in October, I boarded a plane to Virginia, packing the book by Barbara Hurd that Rockwell had asked me to read before coming. It was called *Entering the Stone: On Caves and Feeling Through the Dark.* A month earlier I had opened it with great anticipation, expecting Hurd to tell me how unreasonable my fears of caving were. Instead, she convinced me that even my list of reasonable fears was too short.

I had heard of night terrors but never of cave terror, which was what Hurd experienced the first time she tried caving. She was a teacher of creative writing at the time, working at a camp for young environmentalists. Their program included a field trip to a nearby cave in a couple of days, so she was warming them up by telling them stories about Plato's cave, pointing out how often caves are used as literary symbols of rebirth. The subject of claustrophobia did not come up, though the description of the trip mentioned that a "belly-squirm" would be necessary to make it through the narrow opening to the cave.

When the day finally came, she and her eleven students followed their two guides down the rope ladder, which ended in a muddy pit about ten feet deep and ten feet across. The mouth of the cave was knee high—fairly round and tidy, Hurd said, like a railroad tunnel on a miniature train track. She paid close attention to what the guide said about how to get through the tunnel: head first, then "scooch with your elbows." At the far end, he said, the tunnel would open up on a ledge. Once everyone had crawled down from it into the big room below, they would be able to stand up and stretch.

"The trouble started as soon as I bent down and peered into the chute's entrance," Hurd wrote. She hung back as she watched one kid after another disappear headfirst down the passage. When she was the only one left standing in the pit, the last guide asked her if she was ready to go.

"Yep," she said without moving.

"You okay?" he asked her.

"Yep," she lied again. Then she dropped to her hands and knees and lowered herself down to her elbows so she could fit her head into the tunnel. Dragging herself forward as she had been told to do, she watched the light cast by her headlamp grow smaller and smaller as the tunnel got darker and darker. When she was all the way in, something started moving toward her, fast and loud—maybe wind, she said, maybe sound, but then something else—the Mack truck that had slammed into her cousin's car moments before he died.

Where had that come from? Panicking, she backed out of the cave as fast as she could, forcing the guide behind her to do the same thing. When she reached the pit, she stood up, grabbed hold of the rope ladder, and did not pause to take a deep breath until she was standing at the top in the sunlight again.

Nothing the guide said could convince her to give it another try. She would just wait for the students and let them tell her about it, she said, so the guide left her there with plenty of time to think about what had just happened. She did not believe it was claustrophobia. As a child, she had loved hiding in tight spaces. Had it been a hallucination? She did not know. For years afterward, she had no explanation for her cave terror, but she did figure out that the only way to find out more about it was to try caving again—to enter another stone.

Since I was already committed to my own caving trip, I read the rest of her book like a survival manual, taking notes as I went. Never go caving without at least three sources of light, she said. Always take extra water, and go with an experienced guide. A "squeeze" is a passage so tight that it can scrape the buttons off your clothes and the skin off your face, as evidenced by the names of some of the most famous ones: Gun Barrel, Jam Crack, Electric Armpit Crawl, Devil's Pinch.

When you are stuck in one, the best thing to do is to study the rock. Since it is not letting you go anywhere, you might as well pay attention to where you are. How tight is the squeeze, exactly? Where on your body do you feel it most acutely? Is the floor underneath you sandy or muddy? You still have a light, so use it. What is the color of the stone in this squeeze—is it gray or brown, solid or striped?

In the Buddhist view, even panic can be instructive. Wasn't that what I taught students in my world religions class? Learn to watch your thoughts, I coached those who wanted to meditate. Notice how your mind leaps from thought to thought, creating emotions as it goes. Pay attention to which thoughts give rise to which feelings, and what causes them to recede again. Do not judge yourself, and do not forget to breathe. Rehearsing all this in my mind, I realized how entirely theoretical it was. There was no telling whether it would work if I got stuck in an actual squeeze.

On the night I arrived in West Virginia, Rockwell and Marrion assured me that even though we were headed into a wild cave in the morning, the rooms we were exploring would all be large. They were part of Organ Cave, a complex that includes almost forty miles of cave in a county with more than a thousand caves. Although people have been exploring Organ since 1704, there are still more than two hundred passages in it that no one has ever entered. Soldiers used it for shelter and the manufacture of ammunition during the Civil War. Today it is the eighth longest cave in the country.

As Rockwell talked about his decades of exploring Organ Cave, I stopped him to define terms. A "duck-under" is a passage full of water that is large enough to pass through but only by lying on your back and keeping your nose in the slim airspace at the top. A "sump" is a passage entirely filled with water, leaving no airspace at all. To get through one of those, you have to hold your breath and hope that the passage is not very long. A "virgin cave" is a cave where no one has ever been. Strange things can happen on the way back from one of those, Rockwell said, which are hard to explain once you are back in the light. While he declined to go into detail that night, he said that cavers make a distinction between "friendly" and "unfriendly" caves, and they can usually agree on which is which. Organ Cave is widely regarded as a friendly cave.

Rockwell said he could find a squeeze for me if I really wanted one, but otherwise a belly-squirm was not on our agenda. Instead of feeling relieved, I felt oddly disappointed. I had wanted to compare my experience with Hurd's, to find out if there was a Mack truck inside me too, just waiting for the right conditions to come barreling out of the darkness. Instead I reread her first chapter before I went to bed, wondering why so many of my dreams took place in attics but never in caves.

There was no time to pursue this or any other line of thought once the practicalities of preparation began the next morning. First I got dressed, adding a thin cotton top and jeans over a full layer of thermal underwear. Then the jeans came back off again so I could try on the electric blue coveralls that I would be wearing inside the cave, both to keep me dry and to protect my skin. When it came time to put them on later, I wanted to know my way around.

They were loaners that belonged to my hosts' six-foot-one son-in-law. After everything was zipped up, there was still room for me and someone else in there. Walking over to the mirror to take a look, I was alarmed by how loud my pants were. The fabric was so stiff that when my legs rubbed against each other, they made a sound like a plastic rake on a sidewalk. Looking in the mirror, I saw someone who could have been a well-dressed garbage worker or an astronaut from a poor country. I tried to practice nonchalance, but the suit fought me all the way. It was a business suit, and it furthermore knew more about that business than I did. The suit had been in caves. The suit knew what it was doing. I decided to stop trying to wear the suit and let the suit wear me.

After taking it off, I joined Rockwell and Marrion on the front porch, where gear covered the surface of a large picnic table: helmets, headlamps, batteries, metal water bottles, knee-pads, rubberized gloves, and something called a "sit-upon"— basically, a foam-rubber stadium seat to keep your butt from getting cold if you plan to sit in a cave for a long time. I chose the things that fitted me best and filled my backpack with them, adding an extra headlamp, a thermal top, a wool cap, a Fuji apple, my cell phone and wallet. My sense of foreboding grew as we loaded everything into Rockwell's Toyota 4Runner. When the wind blew, the tree overhead let go a bunch of walnut pods that hit the roof of the car, the ground, and my shoulder like small missiles. I grabbed my helmet and ducked inside the car.

After all that preparation, the drive to the cave only took a few minutes. Outside, it was fully October, with the maples gone all golden and rosy, dropping their leaves on the windshield of the car as we drove. When we arrived, the parking lot was empty except for an orange cat with no tail. We parked across from an old limekiln and a climbing wall with a "for sale" sign in front of it. The gift shop stood next to that, a wooden cabin with a short flight of steps up to a wide porch.

At dinner the night before, Rockwell and Marrion had filled me in on the woman who was coming down the steps to greet us. When the cave came up for auction a few years back, her family had placed the winning bid. They still ran a big cattle farm in the county a couple of miles away, but she ran the cave, selling tickets to the tourists and welcoming the school groups that came on field trips. She knew Rockwell as an experienced caver, which was why she gave him the key to a gate that separated the show part of Organ Cave from the almost forty miles of wild cave that lay beyond.

Organ Cave had something for everyone—a Civil War display for the historians, shallow pools full of microscopic life for the biologists, and exposed rock for the geologists, though the owners of the cave put no stock in evolution. Like most people in the area, they were conservative Christians who embraced the story of creation told in the Bible. According to a brochure I found in the gift shop, Organ Cave was created at the same time as every other cave on earth, after the waters of the deep were opened and moved through the earth before God separated the seas from the dry land.

After we had suited up, tested our lamps, and put on our backpacks, the three of us clumped along the wooden walkway to the mouth of the cave—a huge opening like the mouth of a whale, with vines hanging from its top lip. Looking down, I could see the tree trunks and branches left on the floor of the cave from past floods. After that, the light fell off gradually but steadily. It was like looking at all the levels of light between day and night stacked against each other like sheets of darkening glass.

Hurd had written about this twilight zone in her book. It is where cave dwellers and cave strangers meet, though some can go no farther out and some can go no farther in—or at least not for long. I was one of the cave strangers, whose eyes are not adapted to darkness and who cannot live on the food a cave provides, but who are drawn to caves for our own reasons. Bears come to hibernate and give birth, bats and frogs to escape the heat, raccoons and skunks to take shelter from the weather. Why do humans come? That is harder to say. We come to see what is here and to discover who we are in the presence of what we find.

At the mouth of the cave, we mingle with the cave lovers—earthworms, cave crickets, salamanders, and spiders, which can spend their whole lives here if they want. Plenty of them depend on what cave strangers bring to the cave. When a raccoon leaves a half-eaten mouse behind, it provides a feast for the crickets and beetles that will come out of the darkness after it has gone. When a caver leaves a crust of bread behind, he gives a ghostly fungus a body on which to bloom.

This twilight zone is the place of exchange, Hurd says, not only in terms of food but also in terms of psyche. On this threshold between dark and light, it is still possible to go either way: farther in or back out. It is still possible to see what you are about to lose. Now that I am in the mouth of the whale, I look back at the bright circle of the day, fringed with green vines and shot full of light. When the wind blows, gold leaves drift down. Branches creak and birds call. Turning back to face the cave again, I see only gray: gray stone, gray shadow, gray space. There is no music here, no warmth or food. But I did not come for any of those. I came for the dark, and there is plenty of that.

Or there will be. Right now I am still in the twilight zone, which is part of the show cave. There is a level path under my feet, a metal handrail, and an electric light every six feet so I can see where I am going. According to the map, this is the Chapel Room, where the Confederate soldiers who once took shelter in this cave met for worship. The owners have tried to make this piece of history more vivid by dressing some

mannequins in Civil War uniforms and placing them strategi-
cally throughout the twilight zone. One is standing on a high
rock addressing the invisible troops; another is kneeling with
hands raised in prayer.

Following the path a little farther, I follow Rockwell and
Marrion into the unlit Hopper Room, where more mannequins stand behind old wooden hoppers once used for har-
vesting the saltpeter in this cave for ammunition. The hoppers
are fine, but the mannequins are creepy, not only because they
have gone without dusting for a long time but also because
they are all females, with bushy auburn beards glued to their
faces. Rockwell tells me that this is where we will practice sitting in the dark for the first time.

After we have all chosen our spots, we turn out our headlamps and let the dark have us. The eclipse is total. There is
no light coming from the Chapel Room. There are no dimly
glowing numbers on a watch. There is no moon. This is what
people mean when they say, "It was so dark that I couldn't
see my hand in front of my face." The difference between this
darkness and the darkness of Dialogue in the Dark is that no
one is talking me through this one. There is nothing to listen
to or touch to compensate for the loss of sight.

Rockwell and Marrion are so good at this that I cannot
even hear them breathing. There is not a sound to be heard
in this cave. My ears are as blind as my eyes. Up to now, the
quietest I have ever been was the Sinai desert, where I sat in
silence so thick that it felt like a presence. It was completely

alien and completely comforting at the same time, like being back in my mother's womb only quieter, since I could not hear the beat of her heart or the bellows of her lungs. I could hear mine like never before, but beyond that all I could hear was nothing—nothing for so long that when I finally heard an airplane approaching, I looked up to see a desert fly coming at me instead. Once it had roared over my head with full Doppler effect, the sound of its wings grew fainter and fainter until I could not see it anymore.

After that, I listened to more nothing until I could hear something that sounded like the hum of a high-voltage wire. Since there was no wire for miles around, the sound was obviously coming from inside of me. Through trial and error, I learned that I could make it louder by clenching my jaws and softer by letting them go again, but nothing could make it stop altogether. I had never heard my life before, but that was what it was. It was the sound of my life in the silence of the desert.

Years later, I would hear the American composer John Cage describe the same thing. Famous for exploring silence as seriously as he did sound, he once isolated himself in a soundproof chamber at Harvard so he could experience true and complete silence. When he noticed two distinct sounds in the room—one high and one low—he asked the sound technician what they were. The higher one is your nervous system, the soundman told him, and the lower one is your circulation.

The experience gave both his life and his music direction, Cage said, by introducing him to the concept of nonintention.

His body made sounds without any intention on his part. What might his music sound like if he allowed it to proceed by nonintention too? "I did not know immediately what I was doing," he wrote, "nor, after all these years, have I found out much. I compose music. Yes, but how? I gave up making choices. In their place I put the asking of questions."[1]

Back in the cave, I do not know what I am doing either, but I like it. There is no way to tell time, which means there is no rush. There is no light, which means that I do not have to worry about how I look. There is no one beside me, which means that I do not have to come up with something to say. Above all, there is no threat. Nothing in the Hopper Room frightens me. I do not know what to make of that yet; I have not been in the cave long enough. Like Cage, I think I will give up making choices for a while and let asking questions take its place.

What makes darkness frightening to some people and not to others? What makes it frightening sometimes and not other times? How can cavers tell the difference between a friendly cave and an unfriendly one? Does having a light make a real difference, or is it a security blanket? One thing I am sure of is that being in a cave with people who know what they are doing is the only way to go. Being in this cave alone is not something I want to think about.

Rockwell speaks quietly into the darkness. "I'm going to turn my light on in a minute," he says, making me wonder how many minutes we have been sitting there. "You turn yours on when you're ready and we'll move on." After I have unfolded myself, I head back toward the sound of his voice in the dark, arriving just as he and Marrion turn on their lamps. They are sitting on the same rock, leaning against each other like sweethearts.

Soon after we leave the Hopper Room, we come to an iron gate blocking the passage ahead, the solid dividing line between the show cave behind us and the wild cave ahead. Rockwell fishes around for the key, finds it, and fits it into the ancient-looking lock. When the gate swings open, Marrion and I follow him through. Then he locks it behind us, leaving behind the level path, the handrail, and the electric lights. That is when I imprint on him like a duckling on a duck. *Whither thou goest I will go.*

Our headlamps light a tunnel wide enough for all three of us to walk abreast and high enough that none of our helmets scrapes. I have gotten so used to the sound of my loud overalls that I hardly notice the *skritch-skritch* they make as I walk. The noise makes no difference to the small bats that hang from the low ceiling. I get so close to one that it opens its sleepy eyes to look at me, then pulls the velvet cape of its wing higher so that the eyes disappear from view. As we walk, Rockwell points out some alcoves on the wall of the tunnel where it is still possible to see soot left by the Civil War candles that lit the tunnel more than century ago. Other, smaller tunnels disappear into darkness on our left and on our right.

A little farther on, he stops in front of a left-turning branch that begins with a steep uphill climb. He goes first so he can give Marrion and me a hand up. This is when I come to a full appreciation of my annoying clothes. The treads of the heavy boots find footholds where lesser shoes would have slid right off. The knee pads mean that I can scramble over sharp rocks with no pain, and the overalls work like a second skin that takes all the beating while I stay warm and dry inside.

After I have clawed my way up the chute, we meet in a huge room. Since my headlamp is only good for a few feet in any direction, I cannot see that it is huge, but I can feel that it is huge. The energy of this room is spacious—both alive and vast—like a ballroom before a ball, already gearing up for what is about to happen inside it.

Rockwell walks ahead, while Marrion and I turn aside to look at something round and white that shows up at the edge of our circles of light. It is a bloom of white mold, big and round as a giant dandelion, which has latched onto some leaves left from the last flood—manna in the wilderness, as far as the mold is concerned, since organic matter is hard to find this deep in the cave.

Rockwell suggests that we sit down for another spell in the dark. After we have all found our spots and turned off our lamps, I take in three long breaths while I try to find words for the smell of the cave. Damp shale. Leaf mold. Groundwater. Presence of bat. As much as I do not want to be here alone, my reliance on my hosts allows me to ignore things that matter. When we arrived in this large room, Rockwell put a fluorescent marker down where we entered so we could find the way back out again. When Hurd failed to do that, her teacher corrected her. "In a cave," she told Hurd, "always, always look back. Every few minutes, turn around. Nothing looks the same coming out as it did going in, so you have to memorize the backsides of every boulder, the shape of the hole you've just come through, see the reverse of every angle of slope."[2]

Since my lamp is off, I think about how many hours I have spent in therapy instead, doing more or less the same thing: walking around the boulders of my childhood to see how they look from every angle, peering down into the holes where I spent months in the dark, wondering why the handholds I can see from the top were invisible from the bottom. The difference between the therapy and the cave is that the therapy wants me to look back so I can find another way out, not so I can return by the same way I came. Maybe that makes the cave more like a labyrinth. As long as you stay on the path, you cannot get lost—in time, maybe, but not in space. The path is circular. The way out is the way in. The path, like the cave, never changes. It is literally set in stone. Only the walker changes, not by looking back but by moving ahead, trusting the path to teach her what she needs to know.

While I am deciding whether a cave is more like a labyrinth or a maze, I remember something else Hurd's teacher said: "No romantics in the cave, and no showoffs either. In a cave they're a pain in the ass."[3] Rockwell chooses this moment to end our second session in the dark. Turning on our lamps again, we walk deeper into Organ Cave without talking, large room opening onto larger room until I cannot say whether we have been walking for an hour, two hours, or half a day. When we reach a room that narrows at the end, with a ceiling that slants down instead of up, Rockwell and Marrion slow their pace across the rubble underfoot.

"May I go ahead?" I ask.

"Sure," Rockwell says. "And when you find a place you like, sit down and turn off your lamp. When we see yours go out, we'll turn ours off too. This will be our long sit, the last one of the day."

I go on until I cannot hear their voices anymore, feeling like a child testing her boundaries. The walls draw in closer the farther I go. The ceiling drops lower until the whole room ends at the opening of a low tunnel ringed with rocks. Is this the cave's birth canal? It looks like a good stopping place. When I reach up to turn off my lamp, I see something impossibly sparkly just above my head and stand up to get a better look. It is a long thin fissure in the rock that is full of tiny crystals, every one of them catching the light and tossing it back and forth. What better souvenir of my day in the cave? I aim my headlamp at some pieces that have broken off, choose the one with the most glitter in it, and put it in my backpack before turning off the lamp and sitting down in the dark.

This time I think about all the great spiritual leaders whose lives changed in caves. Gautama Buddha meditated regularly in them, setting such an example for his followers that if you go to India, China, or Tibet, your tour guide can almost always take you to a meditation cave. In Bhutan, you may even be invited to prostrate yourself in front of a niche in the wall where a great master once sat, hollowing out the rock by the force of his consciousness alone.

Muhammad spent a lot of time in a small mountain cave two miles outside of Mecca, where he meditated and prayed for days at a time. On what has become known as the Night of Power, the angel Gabriel came to him there.

"Recite!" Gabriel said.

"Recite what?" Muhammad asked, and Gabriel told him, so the first verses of the Qur'an spooled into the world from the belly of a cave.

Jesus was born in a cave and rose from the dead in a cave. Like most Westerners, I always thought of the stable in Bethlehem as a wooden lean-to filled with straw, at least until I went to the Church of the Nativity in the West Bank. There I learned that caves made the best stables in Jesus's day—no wind whistling through the boards, no predators sneaking up on you from behind. The traditional place of Jesus's birth is not *in* the Church of the Nativity but *under* it, in a small cave under the altar.

The cave in which he rose from the dead is long gone, covered over by the huge Church of the Holy Sepulchre in Jerusalem. Today visitors stand in line to enter a mausoleum that looks nothing like a hole in the ground. This may be just as well, since no one knows for sure what happened there. By all accounts, a stone blocked the entrance to the cave so that there were no witnesses to the resurrection. Everyone who saw the risen Jesus saw him *after*. Whatever happened in the cave happened in the dark.

As many years as I have been listening to Easter sermons, I have never heard anyone talk about that part. Resurrection is always announced with Easter lilies, the sound of trumpets, bright streaming light. But it did not happen that way. If it happened in a cave, it happened in complete silence, in absolute darkness, with the smell of damp stone and dug earth in the air. Sitting deep in the heart of Organ Cave, I let this sink in: new life starts in the dark. Whether it is a seed in the ground, a baby in the womb, or Jesus in the tomb, it starts in the dark.

After that, I stop thinking. I simply sit in the sweet, enveloping darkness, letting it erase me in the best possible way.

When it is time to go, I follow Rockwell and Marrion back out of the cave again, thinking about what good guides they are. They kept me safe while letting me practice courage. They pointed me in the right direction without telling me what to see. Though they have been here many times before, they let me explore my own cave. Maybe that is the difference between pastoral counselors and spiritual directors. We go to counselors when we want help getting out of caves. We go to directors when we are ready to be led farther in. I hope I can remember that the next time someone comes to me with a cave problem. The way out is the way in.

Before long we are back at the gate that separates the two kingdoms of this cave: the one that tourists see and the one that pilgrims see. Opening the gate and then locking it behind us, Rockwell steps aside so Marrion and I can follow the clearly marked way back to the mouth of the cave. Along the way, we pass some college students dipping their test tubes into a shallow pond to see what kind of life they can fish up. The closer we get to the entrance, the more colors I see—first brown, then green, then yellow—then the blue of the brilliant October sky, round as an "O" at the top of the stairs.

Back in my room that night, I unpack my backpack, surprised to find the stone at the bottom. Remembering how it glittered in the darkest part of the cave, I hold it under the reading lamp anticipating miniature fireworks. Instead, it looks like a piece of road gravel—pigeon colored, with a faint sparkle along one side. If I tossed it in my driveway, no one would even lean down to pick it up. What in the world made me think this was a precious stone?

But the stone is not the problem. The light is the problem. Even the reading light is too much. Rummaging in my pack for a penlight, I click it on and aim the beam at my hand. The stone turns into a diamond factory before my eyes, fully as dazzling as I remember. If I were small enough to walk into the opening in this rock, I would walk on a crystal carpet, with a crystal ceiling above my head. The stone is alive with light, but only in the dark. When I turn on the lamp again, it goes back to being a small piece of gravel in my hand.

Or my eyes go back to seeing it that way. When I entered the cave hoping for a glimpse of celestial brightness, it never occurred to me that it might be so small. But here it is, not much bigger than a mustard seed—everything I need to remember how much my set ideas get in my way. While I am looking for something large, bright, and unmistakably holy, God slips something small, dark, and apparently negligible in my pocket. How many other treasures have I walked right by because they did not meet my standards? At least one of the day's lessons is about learning to let go of my bright ideas about God so that my eyes are open to the God who is. Wild or not, God is a cave I do not want to miss.

Before turning off the light, I wrap the treasure I have brought back from my walk in the dark in a red kerchief and tuck it into my luggage so I will not forget it in the morning. It is all I have left of the cave, and it is enough.

The Dark Night
of the Soul

Stand still. The trees ahead and bushes beside you
Are not lost. Wherever you are is called Here,
And you must treat it as a powerful stranger,
Must ask permission to know it and be known.
—David Wagoner

Like darkness itself, the dark night of the soul means different things to different people. Some use the phrase to describe the time following a great loss, while others remember it as the time leading up to a difficult decision. Whatever the circumstances, what the stories have in common is their description of a time when the soul was severely tested, often to the point of losing faith, by circumstances beyond all control. No one chooses the dark night; the dark night *descends*.

When it does, the reality that troubles the soul most is the apparent absence of God. If God is light, then God is gone. There is no soft glowing space of safety in this dark night. There is no comforting sound coming out of it, reassuring the soul that all will be well. Even if comforting friends come around to see how you are doing, they are about as much help as the friends who visited Job on his ash heap. There is an impenetrability to this darkness that isolates the soul inside it. For good or ill, no one can do your work for you while you are in this dark place. It has your name all over it, and the only way out is through.

What can this mean? For some people, it means that it is time to see a good doctor who can help right the mysterious chemistry in the brain. Anyone on a spiritual path needs help from time to time in telling the difference between divine disturbance and mental disorder. It can also help to learn the different tones of voice that your fear uses to warn you away from something. Mine has one voice it uses when it simply does not want to be bothered by anything that may upset my equilibrium. It has another, in a much lower range, that it uses when I am about to walk off the end of a dock. Both can be useful during a dark night, though they are not always easy to tell apart.

When the dark night first falls, it is natural to spend some time wondering if it is a test or punishment for something you have done. This is often a sly way of staying in control of the situation, since the possibility that you have caused it comes with the hope that you can also put an end to it, either by passing the test or by enduring the punishment. The darker possibility—that this night is beyond your control—is often too frightening to consider at first, at least partly because it means that none of your usual strategies for lightening up is going to work. One of the hardest things to decide during a dark night is whether to surrender or resist. The choice often comes down to what you believe about God and how God acts, which means that every dark night of the soul involves wrestling with belief.

I should probably stop here and spend some time talking about the difference between faith and belief, certainty and trust. It might also be helpful to clarify what I mean when I say "God." But since a dark night calls all such definitions into question, it might just be a waste of time. There is also the problem I mentioned earlier: the more ideas we have about how a dark night does or does not operate, the more we will blind ourselves to what is really happening.

The widely acknowledged master of this night is John of the Cross, a sixteenth-century monk whose best-known work is *The Dark Night of the Soul,* begun during the eleven months he spent in a monastery prison.

John was a small man, less than five feet tall. When Teresa of Ávila first met him, she called him "half a friar." Like her, he was a Carmelite, a member of a religious order that had been founded on the ideals of a simple life spent in solitude and prayer. By the time Teresa and John joined the order, the flame of that vision had all but gone out. Some two hundred nuns lived in Teresa's convent, the wealthiest in suites of rooms that they shared with relatives and servants. Though the sisters continued in prayer, they spent very little time in silence or solitude. When Teresa decided to start a new convent closer to the original Carmelite ideal, she faced huge opposition both from the sisters and from their male superiors. She pressed on in spite of it, founding the Monastery of Saint Joseph in Ávila in 1562.

Teresa knew that her reform would fail unless it involved monks as well, so she began to pray for a male ally who could help her found reform monasteries for men. John of the Cross was the answer to her prayers. Twenty-seven years her junior, he became her willing apprentice, and before long the two of them had founded the first house of a new reformed Carmelite order for men. In 1572 John became spiritual director for the nuns at Teresa's original Convent of the Incarnation. Their success did not go unnoticed by the Carmelites who opposed the changes John and Teresa were making. Three years later, when John's superiors told him to quit his job at the convent, he refused, becoming an outlaw to his own order.[1]

On the night of December 2, 1577, men broke into John's room at the Convent of the Incarnation, abducted him and another friar, and led them bound and blindfolded to a monastery in Toledo. When John refused to renounce his work with

Teresa, he was beaten and thrown into the monastery prison, where he survived on little more than bread and water. He was not allowed to bathe or change his clothes. He was not permitted to leave his cell, except for the "circular discipline" of being flogged by other monks.

After two months, John was placed in solitary confinement, where the only light he saw came through a slit in his prison wall. It was there that he began to compose his greatest works—first by memorizing the words in the dark and later, thanks to a kind jailer, by writing them down. When he escaped after nine months, he fled to the south of Spain, where the reformed Carmelites were freer from persecution. There he continued to write down what he had learned in the dark.

Most people who hear the name of John's best-known work assume that it is the memoir of a survivor describing the worst period of his life. Because so many of them have been programmed to think of "dark" as a synonym for "sinister," they open *The Dark Night of the Soul* expecting John to tell them how awful it was and how he got through it by hanging on to his faith in God no matter what happened to him.

Such readers are bound to be disappointed for any number of reasons. In the first place, John does not have much to say about religion. His language is passionate and speaks directly to the senses. For him, the dark night is a love story, full of the painful joy of seeking the most elusive lover of all. In the second place, he is no help at all to anyone seeking a better grip on God. One of the central functions of the dark night, he says, is to convince those who grasp after things that God cannot be grasped. In John's native Spanish, his word for God is *nada*. God is no-thing. God is not a thing. And since God is not a thing, God cannot be held on to. God can only be encountered as that which eclipses the reality of all other things.

In theological terms, this makes John a teacher in the negative way, which does not mean that he is a pain to be around. It means that he does not try to teach by saying what God *is*, since positive statements about God serve chiefly to fool people into believing that their half-baked images of God and their flawed ideas about how God acts are the Real Thing. John works in the opposite direction. He teaches by saying what God *is not*, hoping to convince his readers that their images of and ideas about "God" are in fact obstacles between them and the Real Thing. If this is a disappointment to some of John's readers, it comes as a great relief to others.

I cannot say for sure when my reliable ideas about God began to slip away, but the big chest I used to keep them in is smaller than a shoebox now. Most of the time, I feel so ashamed about this that I do not own up to it unless someone else mentions it first. Then we find a quiet place where we can talk about what it is like to feel more and more devoted to a relationship that we are less and less able to say anything about.

The slippage started with the language of faith, which I had spoken fluently for a long time. After years of teaching other people what words like "sin," "salvation," "repentance," and "grace" really meant, those same words began to mean less and less to me. When I had first learned them, they had helped me to make sense of the tumult both inside and outside, giving me special names for what was happening as well as a sturdy framework for managing it. Then, so gradually that it is hard to say when things changed, those same words began to sound more like stuffed pillows—things to be placed between a person and the hard bones of life so that less bruising occurred. Although I knew what "sin" meant, there were other words with more nuance in them that struck with more force: "betrayal," "brokenness," "forgetfulness," "deadly distance from the source of all life." I could never figure out what made these words less meaningful to people of faith than the word "sin," but they noted the difference. "Why can't you just say 'sin'?" But I had questions of my own. When had the language of faith stopped offering a handle on lived experience and become a container for it instead? Wasn't that like asking God to act inside a box?

Once the words began to break off, the landslide was hard to stop. Remember when you said the Nicene Creed without even thinking about it? Remember when you memorized scripture not as a useful metaphor or a meaningful relic of first-century faith but as a direct revelation of God's own truth? Once you have emerged from whatever safe religious place you were in—recognizing that your view of the world is one worldview among many, discovering the historical Jesus, revolutionizing your understanding of scripture, and updating your theology—once you have changed the way you do church, or at least changed the music at your church and hired a pastor who tweets, or you can no longer find any church within a fifty-mile radius in which you can let down your guard long enough to pray; once the Dalai Lama starts making as much sense to you as the pope or your favorite preacher, and your rare but renovating encounters with the Divine reduce all your best words to dust, well, what's left to hold on to?

I do not believe I am describing a loss of faith in God here. Instead, I believe I am describing a loss of faith in the system that promised to help me grasp God not only by setting my feet on the right track but also by giving me the right language, concepts, and tools to get a hook in the Real Thing when I found it. To lose all that is not the same thing as spending eleven months in a dungeon. It may not even qualify as a true dark night of the soul, but it is without doubt the cloudiest evening of the soul I have known so far. After so many years of trying to cobble together a way of thinking about God that makes sense so that I can safely settle down with it, it all turns to *nada*. There is no permanently safe place to settle. I will always be at sea, steering by stars. Yet as dark as this sounds, it provides great relief, because it now sounds truer than anything that came before.

While the dark night of the soul is usually understood to descend on one person at a time, there are clearly times when whole communities of people lose sight of the sun in ways that unnerve them. This seems to be what is happening to a lot of church people right now, especially those in denominations that are losing members at an alarming rate. While they experiment with new worship styles and set up Facebook pages, most of them know that the problem runs deeper than that. The old ways of being Christian are not working anymore, not even for those who are old themselves. Something in the ways has died, or is dying—truly cause for great sorrow, even among those who know the time has come—and yet at the same time something is being born. Many people refer to the new ways as "emerging Christianity," though there are so many varieties of it that it defies description. The one thing most emerging Christians will say is that the faith they inherited from their elders is all worn out.

Religious scholars register this shift as the tip of a major iceberg. Karen Armstrong says that we are living through a time of global transformation, when religions around the world are taking stock of what enmity has cost them and turning toward some new wisdom about what it means to be fully human.[2] Phyllis Tickle says that we are in the midst of a great rummage sale that the Christian church holds from time to time. Every age has its own accumulation to deal with, along with its own reasons for deciding what stays and what goes. Is substitutionary atonement still useful? How about salvation by faith in Christ alone? Do we really need professional clergy? What about those nineteenth-century hymns? Through it all, the timing remains pretty predictable. In Tickle's terms, what many of us are taking part in, willingly or not, is Christianity's "semi-millennial rummage sale of ideas."[3] The last one was called the Protestant Reformation. No one knows what to call this one yet.

In his book *The Future of Faith*, Harvey Cox says that the Age of Belief ended in 2005, when the new European Union declined to mention "Christian" anywhere in its constitution.[4] People have voted with their feet. Doctrines and creeds are no longer enough to keep faith alive. Instead, the faithful seek practical guidance and direct experience of the sacred. The new age we are living in is the Age of the Spirit, Cox says, already well under way in the global South.

If this is a liberating moment for some people of faith, it is a moment of profound loss for others. Maybe you do not get one without the other, but age makes a difference. If I were twenty-five years old, just beginning to find my place in this great emergence, my excitement level would be higher than it is at sixty, when it seems likely that I will not live long enough to see what emerges. At my age I am supposed to be invested in bonds, not stocks. There is not enough time left to plant trees that take a long time to grow.

Recently I picked up the thirty-fifth printing of a book that was first published in 1981, James Fowler's *Stages of Faith*.[5] It was required reading in seminary, and though a lot of things have happened to change the world since then—the AIDS epidemic, the World Wide Web, 9/11—Fowler's stages still sound familiar: the fantasy-filled, imitative faith of early childhood, followed by the more literal faith of schoolchildren; then the conventional faith of adolescence, largely inherited, followed by the individuated faith of young adulthood. Plenty of people stop there, he says, while others go on to stages he finds harder and harder to describe.

At the fifth stage, which Fowler says is unusual before midlife, people know "the sacrament of defeat." They live with the consequences of choices they cannot unchoose. They have been permanently shaped by commitments they cannot unmake. Yet there is still a lot of undoing at this stage, as people let go of many of the certainties about themselves and the world that they earlier worked so hard to put in place. The boundaries of the tribe no longer hold. Strangers and strange truths are no longer frightening but compelling. Paradoxical truths are the most compelling of all. With the gravitas that arrives when life is more than half over, people at this stage are ready to spend and to be spent, emptying their pockets in one last-ditch effort to make meaning.

Earlier I declined to define my terms, but Fowler does a good job of defining his. Religion, faith, and belief are not the same thing, he says, though we often speak of them as if they were. In the sixteenth century, "to believe" meant "to set the heart upon," or "to give the heart to," as in, "I believe in love." But in the centuries following the Enlightenment, secular use of the words "belief" and "believe" began to change until they said less about the disposition of one's heart than about the furniture in one's mind. By the nineteenth century, when knowledge about almost anything consisted chiefly of empirical facts, belief became the opposite of knowledge. A person's belief in God was reduced to his or her belief system—the unprovable statements of faith that person judged to be true.

The great pity of this conflation, Fowler says, is that when faith is reduced to belief in creeds and doctrines, plenty of thoughtful people are going to decide that they no longer have faith. They might hang on if they heard the word used to describe trust or loyalty in something beyond the self, but when they hear "faith" used to signify belief in a set formula of theological truths, the light in their eyes goes out.

When I listen to college students talk about faith, beliefs are what interest them most: Do you believe in the virgin birth? Do you believe that Jesus died for your sins? Do you believe that only Christians go to heaven? No one asks, "On what is your heart set?" No one asks, "What powers do you most rely on? What is the hope that gives meaning to your life?" Those are questions of faith, not belief. The answers to them are not written down in any book, and they have a way of shifting in the dark.

"If you have understood, then what you have understood is not God," Saint Augustine said in the fourth century. Sixteen hundred years later, the Northern Irish theologian Peter Rollins says the same thing with equal force. God is an event, he says, "not a fact to be grasped but an incoming to be undergone."[6]

All in all, there have never been a lot of people lining up to learn what God is not—especially not now, with so many self-appointed teachers volunteering to reveal the truth about God to anyone who will hold still long enough to listen. The only people I know who are interested in what God is not are those who have run through all the other answers and found them wanting. Waking up in the middle of their own dark nights, they have come quickly to the end of their intellectual resources—and their Sunday school resources too—so there is nothing to do but lie in the dark with something heavy on their chests, listening for a voice in the darkness that does not come.

If that has ever happened to you, you know how fast it can make you ready to listen to anyone who can tell you what all that *not-ness* is about. John's answer is not simple, but in the simplest possible terms, he says that the dark night is God's best gift to you, intended for your liberation. It is about freeing you from your ideas about God, your fears about God, your attachment to all the benefits you have been promised for believing in God, your devotion to the spiritual practices that are supposed to make you feel closer to God, your dedication to doing and believing all the right things about God, your positive and negative evaluations of yourself as a believer in God, your tactics for manipulating God, and your sure cures for doubting God.

All of these are substitutes for God, John says. They all get in God's way. The late Gerald May, who wrote his own book about John, called them addictions. In many cases, he said, we should give thanks for them, because it is our addiction to some God substitute or another that finally brings us to our knees, by helping us realize how far we have strayed from our heart's true desire.[7]

John knows there is more than one kind of darkness out there. He makes a distinction between *tinieblas,* the kind of darkness you would be wise to turn away from, and *oscura,* which simply means obscure, or difficult to see. Clinical depression should not be mistaken for the dark night, May says, though the two can overlap. Like *tinieblas,* depression can take people apart without putting them back together again, while *la noche oscura* is for healing. To paraphrase another writer on the negative way, when depression passes, all is restored; when the dark night passes, all is transformed.[8]

Yet it would be a mistake to attach the promise of *more* spiritual benefits to a night that is designed to obliterate them. Those who have come through dark nights of their own, not just once but over and over again, often cannot find the words to say why they would not trade those nights for anything. *Yes, they were nights of great loss. Yes, the soul suffered from fearful subtraction. Yes, a great emptiness opened up where I had stored all my spiritual treasures, and yet.* And yet what? *And yet what remained when everything else was gone was more real than anything I could have imagined. I was no longer apart from what I sought; I was part of it, or in it. I'm sorry I can't say it any better than that. There was no place else I wanted to be.*

God puts out our lights to keep us safe, John says, because we are never more in danger of stumbling than when we think we know where we are going. When we can no longer see the path we are on, when we can no longer read the maps we have brought with us or sense anything in the dark that might tell us where we are, then and only then are we vulnerable to God's protection. This remains true even when we cannot discern God's presence. The only thing the dark night requires of us is to remain conscious. If we can stay with the moment in which God seems most absent, the night will do the rest.

May wrote his book on John of the Cross while he was waiting for a heart transplant. Years earlier he had undergone chemotherapy for a cancer that his doctors pronounced cured, though the cure caused the heart disease that took him back to death's door. Since his sickness had brought him closer to God and his loved ones than he had ever been before, May said he finally gave up trying to decide what was ultimately good or bad. "I truly do not know," he wrote. He died in 2005 at the age of sixty-four.

This kind of unknowing is a world away from the kind that causes people to abandon faith. Nicholas of Cusa called it "holy ignorance," a divine gift given to those who are willing to embrace all that they cannot and will never know about the Giver. May said that even near the end he had an abiding sense of God's presence. He could feel it anywhere, anytime, he said, sounding just like Lusseyran. All he had to do was turn his attention toward it.

"I love it and surely would hate to lose it," he wrote. "It's the answer to a very long prayer. But I know it is not God. It is only a sense *of* God. I don't think I make an idol of it, so I don't imagine it will need to be taken away. If at some point I do lose it again, I hope I will be given the wisdom to continue to trust God in the absence of any sense of God."[9]

At this stage of my life, this sounds like a fifth Gospel, in which the good news is that dark and light, faith and doubt, divine absence and presence, do not exist at opposite poles. Instead, they exist with and within each other, like distinct waves that roll out of the same ocean and roll back into it again. As different as they are, they come from and return to the same source. If I can trust that—if I can give my heart to it and remain conscious of it—then faith becomes a verb, my active response to the sacred reality that the best religions in the world can only point to.

This faith will not offer me much to hold on to. It will not give me a safe place to settle. Practicing it will require me to celebrate the sacraments of defeat and loss, but since the religion I know best has a lot to say about losing as the pre-condition for finding, I can live with that. I think I can even live inside this cloudy evening of the soul for a while longer, where even my sense of God's absence can be a token of God's presence if I let it. Because I do not understand a thing about this, does that mean I understand God? I do not know. All I know is that there is no place I would rather be.

Working with Darkness

We cannot live in a world that is interpreted for us
by others. An interpreted world is not a hope.
Part of the terror is to take back our own listening.
To use our own voice. To see our own light.
—Hildegard of Bingen

M y formal study of darkness is coming to an end. Though
I will continue to learn from it for the rest of my life,
I am looking for some way to measure the distance covered.
What is different, now that I have met Jacques Lusseyran and
Miriam Greenspan, now that I have followed Rockwell and

Marrion into Organ Cave, and let John of the Cross teach me about the dark night of the soul? I am ready for my exam.

One night while I am sorting through old magazines, I find a back issue of a Buddhist journal called *Tricycle*. I read a lot of Buddhist writers these days, since they seem to know more about the dazzling dark of human consciousness than my living Christian teachers do. Back in the 1960s, when Thomas Merton and the Dalai Lama invited monks from their respective traditions to meet for dialogue and meditation, they thought it would work since those who have devoted themselves to full-time spiritual practice are often able to meet in the clearing beyond words. Although Merton died before he could write much about this project, he left a prayer that I keep on my bedside table. You can find it at the end of this book.

There is a picture of a sleeping Buddhist monk on the cover of *Tricycle* magazine—sleeping or meditating, I cannot tell which. Underneath the black-and-white photo of his peaceful face is a headline in glow-in-the-dark green:

GREEN MEDITATION
Find Enlightenment in the Dark

The article is by a man named Clark Strand who spent time as a Zen monk. He starts with an assertion that I have by now heard many times: that the invention of the incandescent light-bulb changed life on earth in ways that most human beings remain largely oblivious to. That invention was the spiritual tipping point, he says. By providing us with good, cheap light, the lightbulb allowed us to make advances in every area of human enterprise, convincing us that there was nothing we could not handle with just a little more light.

The only casualty was darkness—"a thing of little value," Strand wrote, "an absence really, a blank space on the canvas of eternity that we could fill in as we pleased. Or so we thought."[1]

Like other insomniacs before him, Strand was drawn to his topic because he could not sleep. For ten years he had been waking up in the middle of the night and lying there for a couple of hours wondering what was wrong with him before drifting back to sleep. In his search for answers, he came across a sleep study conducted at the National Institute of Mental Health, which was how he learned that there was nothing wrong with the way he slept.

Before the invention of the lightbulb, almost no one slept eight hours at a time. That is a modern convention, made possible by an abundance of artificial light. In the long centuries before the advent of electricity, people spent as much as fourteen hours of every day in the dark, which affected their rest as well as their activity. When the researchers at NIMH recruited some of the most normal people they could find to replicate that pattern, those people began to discover states of consciousness that they had never experienced before.

At first they played catch-up, sleeping an average of eleven hours a day. Eventually they settled down to eight hours again, but the hours were not consecutive. With fourteen full hours of darkness available to them, most lay quietly in bed for a couple of hours each night before falling soundly asleep. Four hours later, they woke up and spent another couple of hours resting before falling asleep again. The rest hours turned out to be the most interesting ones to the scientists, since during those hours the sleepers were neither actively awake nor soundly asleep. Their body chemistry hovered somewhere in between, just like their brain waves did.

The director of the study said that it was like finding a fossil of human consciousness, a state of awareness that had largely withered away. In prehistoric times, this rest state may have provided a channel of communication between dreams and waking life, supplying rich resources for myth and fantasy. It may also explain why so many biblical stories are powered by big dreams. But once people learned how to light the night, they began to cut down on the number of hours they spent in darkness every day. Eventually they condensed their sleep as well, compressing it into eight-hour blocks with no lag time in the middle or on either end. Now "a good night's sleep" means seven or more hours of uninterrupted sleep that end when the alarm rings, whether the sun is up or not. The long hours of rest before, during, and after sleep are gone, along with the state of consciousness that went with them—the collateral damage of a world in love with light.

Strand's article has nothing to do with trying to recover primeval patterns of sleep by going off the grid altogether. Instead, he suggests a limited experiment in which those who are interested choose a length of time and a quiet place where they can set darkness and sleep free from artificial light. He recommends a shallow cave if you can find one since that allows the best mix of dark and light, but almost any place will do. A city apartment is nothing but a shallow cave, he points out. The only difference is electricity and a lock.

I know just the place—a small twelve-by-twelve-foot cabin in the woods with no power or plumbing but lots of windows. I also know the time—the summer solstice, coming up in just a few days. Strand has something longer in mind, but the solstice has two things going for it: it sounds important, and it is the shortest night of the year. If my exam does not go well, at least it will not last long.

The basic idea is to let the planets determine how much light there is, retiring sometime before dusk and dark—*before* you are tired—so that you can notice the light change. After a while, Strand says, you may notice that the darkness is "listening" to you. If that happens, you should speak to the darkness about whatever is on your mind. If that makes you self-conscious, you should speak to the darkness about that. "During this time," he adds, "there is nothing whatsoever that you are forbidden to say or think or feel."

Packing is easy. I will not be able to read, so I do not need a book. I will not be able to write, so I do not need paper or pen. I will not have electricity, so I do not need anything that plugs in. I am forgoing artificial light, so I do not need a headlamp. All I really need is a cotton sheet and a bottle of water, which does not seem like nearly enough. With nothing else to do, I pick up my nearly empty duffel and head to the woods.

There is still plenty of light outside, with a good hour to go before sunset. The cabin is an easy ten-minute walk away. About halfway there, I hear a sound behind me and turn around to see my old dog Dancer trailing along behind me. When I look at him, he ducks his head and wags his tail. "Sure, you can come," I say, waiting up for him, glad to have someone other than the dark to talk to.

When I get to the cabin, I spend a while sweeping dead wasps from the floor and opening all eight of the windows. A live scorpion lies stretched out on one of the sills, its tail curled in a perfect question mark. I hope it does not walk in its sleep. A narrow daybed is pushed up against the opposite wall, the futon mattress even with the bottoms of two large windows. The only other furniture in the room is a big red leather chair with brass studs and a matching ottoman that faces a small stone fireplace full of ashes from the previous winter.

Dancer rolls in the leaves outside while I put the sheet on the bed and pile up some pillows. The lingering heat of the day is still considerable, though the canopy of trees overhead shields the cabin from the last of the sun. After checking to make sure that the small battery-powered fan gives off no light, I decide that it is allowed and turn it on to keep the air moving inside. This turns out to be doubly useful since the cabin has been taken over by large black ants. Every time I settle down on the bed, one comes out of the woodwork to explore me. Since this is a Buddhist retreat, I let the ants live. If I keep the fan pointed straight at my body, it blows most of them off before they get very far. It also gives me something to do while I wait for night to fall, watching the light fade through the windows like I am waiting for a drive-in movie to begin.

Just past the glass, the gray trunks of trees are spaced so evenly that they remind me of Irish standing stones, with lichen on them spelling out names I cannot read. Higher up, the last bits of light are making lace of the high limbs of those same trees, while a lone firefly moves through them—first here, then there—showing up in the dusk like a child playing hide-and-seek with a piece of bright clothing hanging out. Meanwhile the cicadas are tuning up for the night. Since they are closest, they are easiest to hear, but I can also hear a distant truck, a barking dog, a hooting owl. I can also hear a woman laughing, which mystifies me since the nearest neighbor lives half a mile away.

The mattress underneath me smells like every camp mattress I ever knew. When the evening breeze arrives at last, it brings other smells along with it: the fragrance of fallen limbs wet from last night's rain, downed trees turning back to topsoil, the slight but sharp tang of pine. The longer I look out the window, the more shapes I see in the leaves above my head. Directly above me there is a rabbit's head. Next to that, there is an owl's mask, and right beside that the face of a billy goat with horns. The leaves do not change shape the way clouds do, but the sky behind them does. When I look at the goat a little later, it has two stars right in the middle of its eyes. A little while after that, the stars have moved down the goat's face like tears. A little while after that, they are in the clear again, looking like nothing but stars.

I have lost track of time and of the dark as well. It is darker than it was, but it is not completely dark. So what do we mean when we say, "It's dark outside"? Clearly, "dark" is a relative term. Do we mean that it is too dark to walk through the house without running into furniture? Do we mean that it is too dark to read without a light? Sometimes all we mean is "This room is not fully lit," as if that were the norm.

My little room is not fully lit, but it is not dark either. Watching the shifting patterns outside the window takes me back to one of the most frightening nights of my life, which also featured a window at the foot of my bed. I was alone in a beautiful house in the woods on a night of deep snow. Everyone else had gone home for the holidays. I was lying in a bed where I knew someone had died several years earlier, though not by violent means. She was extremely fond of the house, from everything I had heard, having spent the best years of her life there.

I was trying not to think too much about that as the hour grew later and still I could not sleep. But clearly I did sleep, since I later woke to the sound of a sharp crack in the hallway. It sounded like someone walking on loose floorboards toward my room—impossible but audible—though as soon as I sat

up the sound stopped. Had it been a creaking rafter? Had a
branch heavy with snow fallen on the roof? When the crack
changed to a shuffle, the fear came on me so fast that I literally
could not move, though I willed myself to stand up and turn
on a light, or call out a question to whatever was in the hallway.
Who are you and what do you want?

The dread of it sat on my chest like a rock. Before long I
was sure I could hear breathing just outside my closed door. I
was also sure that the presence was malign, though it is impossible now to say why. Though closing my eyes was out of the
question, I did not look down for fear I would see something
dark and foggy pushing its fingers under the door. I looked
up instead, in the general direction of God, but God was not
present in any way that helped.

I recited the Lord's Prayer as the next best thing. The
frightening presence outside my door did not come in, and
it did not go away. Whatever power kept it where it was, I
gave thanks with shallow breaths, afraid to make any noise that
might shift the balance. This went on for hours, or at least I
think it did. The clock was on the chest of drawers and I was
pinned to the bed, where the only thing I wanted in the world
was for the sun to come up.

When the room began to lighten, I started to cry. The
weakness of the thing outside my room grew in direct propor-
tion to the light coming in my window. Worshipping the sun
made all kinds of sense to me. While I lay counting the bright-
ening minutes, the dark fog thinned and poured away down

the hall, taking its fingers with it. My chest filled for the first time all night. The paralysis ebbed. I held my hand up in front of my face and practiced breathing in and out while I flexed my fingers. The dark night was over. I had been delivered into the bright light of a new day.

Years later I would meet people, especially young people, who suffered from what their doctors called "night terrors." These are different from nightmares in several ways, as I learned from one family whose daughter had a mild case. The first night they heard her screaming, they found her standing at the door of their room, crying for help while apparently still asleep. Once they succeeded in waking her up, she was confused about why she was in their room instead of hers, but she soon went back to sleep. In the morning she did not remember a thing, though her parents had a hard time forgetting.

When they took her to their family doctor, he had a name for what had happened to their daughter, as well as an explanation. She really was asleep. Night terrors usually affect people during the first three hours of the sleep cycle, when they only partly surface from deep sleep on schedule. Their minds stay down while their bodies come up for air, so that they are able to move and speak without being fully conscious. This makes the experience scarier and more dangerous both for them and for those who live with him. The good news is that most children grow out of the terrors by the age of eight or nine.[2]

Back at the cabin, there is nothing to be afraid of and I am in no hurry to get to sleep, which is why I have time to wonder why most of us put such pressure on ourselves to sleep in regulated ways. Why do so many of us suffer from insomnia that we can name our favorite sleep aids? If you read as many books on "sleep hygiene" as I do, you would learn that normal human sleep includes five or six complete cycles of sleep that move through predictable stages. Normal people wake up four or five times during the night. Some drift back to sleep in seconds while others lie awake for a while. For most of us, the main impediment to getting back to sleep is worrying about getting back to sleep. The older we get, the less sleep we need. Sometimes the fact that you cannot get back to sleep means that you are not tired anymore. There is not a reason in the world why you cannot get up and do something other than lie in bed trying to will yourself back to sleep.

Even if you are a true insomniac, you are in very good company. Famous insomniacs include Benjamin Franklin, Thomas Edison, Charles Dickens, Mark Twain, and Virginia Woolf. Vincent Van Gogh did some of his best work at night, not because he set his alarm clock to get up after dark but because he could not sleep. There were nights he wished he were a believer in God, he confessed, so that he would have someone to beg for sleep, but he was not. "That does not keep me from having a terrible need of—shall I say the word—religion," he wrote in his journal. "Then I go out at night and paint the stars."[3]

Back in the cabin, it must be long after midnight, and still it is not dark. The stars are still moving down the canvas of the sky as the world turns toward morning. Watching the shifting patterns of trees and sky takes me back to my earliest memory, of green vines growing on white latticework that move upward as I watch. When I asked my mother about this, she said I was remembering the outside staircase to the second-floor apartment where we lived when I was six months old. "You could not possibly remember that," she said. But I do.

Tonight I am as close to that infant as I have been in a long time. Like her, I am temporarily illiterate, unable to read or write. I cannot work a light switch or make myself a snack. All I can do is lie here in my crib, watching the shapes change in my darkening room while all the adults are busy elsewhere doing all the purposeful things that adults like to do. The biggest thing that has happened for me in the last hour is that the stars have moved. The biggest thing that will happen for me in the next hour is that the stars will move some more. Maybe I will see them, maybe I won't. They do not need my help. They do not even need a witness, though that is what I have become—a watcher—someone who has set down every purpose except for resting in the dark.

Since my instructions included speaking to the dark while I lie here, I try to think of something to say. "If there is anything you want to show me, here I am," I say, but apparently the stars are the only things on the agenda tonight. After the lesson with the small stone from the cave, I know better than to ask for more. Unless the owl counts. I have never heard this particular one before, shouting three rounds of *hoo-HOO* before trailing off with a fourth *hooooooo* at the end. I practice the call a couple of times so I can look up the bird in the morning, but I am getting drowsy now. The darkness is incredibly soothing—a sense-surround tranquilizer—and lying right next to the screen is like lying in a hammock.

If only the ants would stop. Every time I start to drift off, one of them manifests itself on the back of my knee, the top of my thigh, or the base of my neck, running over my skin like a swami over hot coals. Every time this happens, I fling off the covers, sweep the thing as far away from me as I can, and try to get back to sleep again. At least Dancer has stopped snoring.

Yet for all these minor irritations, there is nothing threatening about this night. It is as far away from my most frightening night as it can be, which leads me to wonder about the difference the next time I wake up. When I do, the sky is still not dark, though the lighter portion that was once in the west has shifted to the east. The woods are quieter now than before, though I can still hear a few late-night crickets and cicadas. I wonder if that is the main difference between this night and the frightening one: there are no people here. There have never been any people here, except for the moonshiners who hid their stills in these woods and a hunter or two during deer season. Am I more afraid of people than I am of the dark?

It is also summer instead of winter, I am lying in my bed instead of someone else's bed, and there is a dog beside me on the floor. Come to think of it, I have never heard a single ghost story that involved a dog. Maybe Dancer makes all the difference? Or maybe this cabin is simply a friendly cave.

One thing this night and the other have in common is the conspicuous absence of God. During the frightening night, I actively pleaded for divine intervention. Here I have simply announced my readiness to listen, but all I hear are the normal sounds of a summer's night in the north Georgia woods. It is not that I expect to hear an actual voice, but I have courted the Beloved long enough to know what it is like to receive a divine visit: it is like coming home after a long time away; it is like being held by someone with all the time in the world; it is like remembering a dream that opens a door. Earlier in my life I wanted more specificity than that. I wanted a divine parent who would give me direct answers, clear guidance, specific tasks. Now that I have accepted responsibility for supplying those things myself, it is enough to step away from them from time to time, resting in the presence of the Beloved who accepts all answers, covers all directions, finishes all tasks.

Tonight it is possible to accept this peaceful darkness as a token of the divine presence, but what about that frightening night? When darkness comes not as a friend but as a threat, then what? I wish I had known John of the Cross and Gerald May that night long ago. In the absence of any sense of God, I wish I had known that it was still possible to trust God. Since I remained conscious, maybe I did. All these years later, when I think back to whatever was snuffling outside my door, I wonder if it was a lost thing or a lonely thing that was looking for some company. It was certainly a dark thing, but that does not mean it was a bad thing. It did not harm me. My fear did that. It did not even open the door, which was not locked. All night long, it sat outside my door waiting for me to decide whether to open up or not, and I decided not—a decision that has come back to haunt me in a whole new way.

Whom did I refuse to let in that night? Did I turn the Beloved away because of a frightening mask? Or was the Beloved out there without a mask for once, asking only that I handle my fear long enough to let the divine darkness in? I will never know. I do not even know what I would do if I had it to do over again. How many times since then have I rejected Love because it did not present itself the way I expected, in a form acceptable to me? I do not know that either. All I know is that I am as rested as I have ever been after my short night in this cloud of unknowing, where I let the darkness manage me for once instead of trying to manage the darkness.

When this last patch of quiet rest ends, the sun is full up. The clock says eight, which means that my twelve-hour Green Meditation Retreat has come to an end. As tired as I am of the ants, I am terribly sad to go. This shallow cave has been good to me. At least I know my way back. The way out is the way in.

I close the windows, gather up my few things.

"Come on, Dancer," I say, and he does, wagging his tail full of leaves.

Our Lady of the Underground

All I want is the moon, Helicon. I know in advance
what will kill me. I have not yet exhausted all that can
make me live. That is why I want the moon.
—Albert Camus

As many times as I have gone out of my way to see a full sunrise, I have never done the same to see a full moonrise. I have caught a few by accident, pulling off the road to avoid wrecking the car while I try to get a better look at the giant golden thing pushing its way up behind the tangle of trees. In the city it appeared through the spaces between buildings, but the effect was no less startling, both because of its size and because nothing on earth could replicate the effect of its light.

Nothing reminds me that I am an earthling like seeing the full moon. Years of Christian training fall at my feet like paper clothes set on fire by the sight. I want to dance and shake a rattle. I want to thank the moon for coming, beg her to show me the world by her light, ask her to tell me stories all night long—and when she grows faint near the first light of day, plead with her not to go, though I know full well she will.

As much as well-meaning Christians have tried to convince me that I cannot love creation with anything close to the love with which I love God, I remain unconvinced. If I am allowed to love the water of baptism, the bread and wine of Communion, the oil of healing, and the wood of the cross, why am I not also allowed to love the heavenly moon? I resolve to watch the last full moonrise of the year.

This takes some planning, since the moon rises on its own schedule instead of mine. I cannot choose the least busy evening of the month to go see it or decide which of several showings to attend on the day. Everything else must be pushed aside to be there when the moon comes up. But where will "there" be? And how will I know where to look?

I decide to watch from the highest point on the land where I live, which is not high enough to see the moon rise without trees in the way but still high enough to see it before the neighbors do. According to the Farmer's Almanac, it will come up at 6:11 P.M. on Friday, December 28, seven days after the winter solstice. That will make it a Sabbath moon as well as a full one. It will have been full since 5:22 A.M. that morning, though not where I could see it. I will only be able to see it when the sun goes down on one horizon and the moon comes up on the other, like one of two bright children on far ends of a teeter-totter.

When the day circled on the kitchen calendar comes, Ed and Dancer go with me, heading into the dusk without a light to find the best place to watch the show. The fescue in the pasture is so tall that none of us moves quickly. Every step requires a high dance step with a slight pause at the top to make sure we do not come down in a yellow jacket nest or a groundhog hole. Every now and then, we come to a matted circle where deer slept last night or the night before. Then it is back into the high grass up the high hill until we are all making steam clouds with our breath.

At the top, we orient ourselves by turning to face the setting sun. Then we turn 180 degrees and search for a glow in the east, but it is too soon to tell exactly where the moon will come up. There are no trees left on the hill where we stand except one elderly white pine. All the others that were here when we arrived twenty years ago are gone now, having fallen to pine borers, old age, and lightning. Only the one is left, a real grandfather of a tree with deep green clouds of needles, a few hanging limbs, and a gnarled trunk leaking sap. We consider sitting down beneath it but cannot sacrifice the view, so we let Dancer decide instead. His hips hurt so bad that he goes down the minute we stop and look at him. I sit where he can lay his head on my lap, and Ed sits behind me so I can lean on him.

There is nothing to hear but our own breathing, unless you count the muted bark of a distant dog or the acceleration of an engine a couple of miles away. The darkness around us is thickening like syrup, though there is not yet a single star visible in the sky. Dancer sighs. I pat his head, and he bangs his tail on the grass. The evening is already so beautiful that it is easy to see why Jews imagine the Sabbath as a bride. When three stars appear, she will arrive. Even now, she fills the space without saying a word. She is present even in her absence, with everyone waiting on tiptoe for a glimpse of her, wanting to be the first to see her and let everyone else know she is here.

And yet the Sabbath is never only about the bride. When she appears, it means the wedding can begin. When she comes through the door, everyone in her presence becomes as rich in God's love as she is. She is the mirror, not the light. As beautiful as she is, she is this night's reminder of every other night like this, when the last day of the week lies down in the grass so the new day of God's own rest can begin—not with light but with darkness. *And there was evening and there was morning, the seventh day.*

In the book of Genesis, darkness was first; light came second. Darkness was upon the face of the deep before God said anything. Then God said "light" and there was light, but the second word God said was not "darkness," because the darkness was already there. How did it get there? What was it made of? I do not know. All I know is that darkness was not created; it was already there, so God's act on the first day of creation was not to make light and darkness but to make light and separate it from the darkness, calling the light "day" and the darkness "night."

If this primordial story of separation plays a role in our problems with darkness, that is because we turn it into a story of opposition by loading it with values that are not in the story itself. Nowhere does it say that light is good and darkness is bad. Nowhere does it say that God separated light and darkness as a test, to see which one human beings would choose. That is the fruit story, not the darkness story.

"How long since we have done this?" Ed says in my ear. How long since we have left our house, which we know so well, to climb a hill and sit next to each other in the dark with nothing to do but wait for the moon to rise? How long since we have sat quietly under such enormous space?

"Twenty years," I say.

"Why is that?" he says.

He and I both know why, but the answer makes me so sad that I cannot say it out loud. We have been busy. For twenty years.

Busy? The word loses all meaning under the canopy of this sky. The horizon in front of us is all treetops except for the roofline of one house a couple of miles away. Since we did not bring a compass, I am not sure where to look. I know where the sun comes up in my kitchen window, but everything looks different up here. The sky is not framed, for one thing. There is a lot more of it, for another.

Then I see it: a thin slice of perfectly round persimmon showing just above the roofline of the house. There is one house on the whole horizon, and that is where the moon comes up?

"Quick!" I say to Ed. "We have to move!"

"Why?" he says, but then he sees it too, and we break Dancer's heart by moving six feet away. At least now we can see the show without the silhouettes of satellite dishes, chimneys, and bathroom vents on the moon. Her face is perfectly round, perfectly orange, perfectly huge. She is the perfect bride, with one bright star shining behind her right shoulder.

After such a long wait, we are both surprised by how fast the moon rises, growing smaller and paler as she climbs into the sky. She is still the loveliest thing I have seen all day, all week, all year. When it becomes apparent that there is no real stopping place—that the three of us could lie here all night or at least until we got so cold that we could not move our fingers or legs—we stand to head back to the house.

Dancer needs help, so we make a sling with our hands to lift him to his feet. Then he staggers after us, back down the hill the same way we came. That is when we discover that we can make the moon rise again and again by changing our position. As we descend, the moon does too, dropping back down behind the ridge of trees. If we wanted, we could sit down every ten feet and watch it rise all over again. This makes it easier to go, somehow, though not without promising to return before twenty more years have passed.

The full moon comes around so regularly that I could circle it on my calendar if I really meant to watch it rise. When I was a parish priest, I learned to use the table in the back of *The Book of Common Prayer* to find the date for Easter every year. That table may well contain the only hard science in the book, but the rule that accompanies it sounds distinctly Druid: "Easter Day is always the Sunday after the full moon that occurs on or after the spring equinox on March 21, a date which is fixed in accordance with an ancient ecclesiastical computation, and which does not always correspond to the astronomical equinox."[1] To find the date in any particular year, one must know both the Golden Number and the Sunday Letter. When I ran my finger down the columns of numbers to plan the following year's church calendar, I always felt as if I should be wearing a wizard's hat instead of a clergy collar.

Yet even a child who came upon the page during a particularly long sermon could not help but notice this: Easter comes on a different day every year. Like Passover, it is tethered to the spring equinox, but on that relatively long leash it may occur anywhere from March 22 to April 25, never falling on the same day two years in a row. This year Easter fell on April 8, 2012. That happened in 2007 as well, but unless the moon slows down or the earth speeds up, it will not happen again until 2091.

If Christians look to creation for wisdom about the spiritual life, seeing resurrection in springtime, divine promise in a rainbow, or the flight of the Spirit in a dove, why don't we look to the moon for wisdom about our relationship to God?

Sometimes the light is coming, and sometimes it is going. Sometimes the moon is full, and sometimes it is nowhere to be found. There is nothing capricious about this variety since it happens on a regular basis. Is it dark out tonight? Fear not; it will not be dark forever. Is it bright out tonight? Enjoy it; it will not be bright forever.

But humans do not easily relinquish our control over how dark or bright it is, either in our houses or in our souls. Add Christian teaching to our natural fear of the dark and the aversion becomes sanctified. At church, we learn that we are called to be children of the light. When we praise the Son, we appreciate the pun. Yes, we praise the Sun too. Giving thanks for good weather, we walk the straightest path we can by the clear light of day. As night approaches, we close our doors against the children of darkness, turning on our security lights and praying to God to keep us safe through all the dangers and perils of the night, for "God is light and in him there is no darkness at all" (1 John 1:5).

It is the dominant view, and there is no sense arguing with it. But for those who have suffered from this division of their days, doing their best to stay on lit paths and avoid dark places without ever quite shaking the sense that they are shutting themselves off from something vital for their souls, there is another way. There is a whole dark night of spiritual treasure to explore.

Although I am not Catholic, I am devoted to Mary. Part of it is that she is a she; the other part is that she is entirely human. Most of the time I think she understands me better than her son does, since she has a whole DNA spiral and a body that operates on a lunar cycle—or did. Even if she has left that part of her life behind now, as I have, she remembers what it was like to fill like the moon every month and then to empty. She knows what it is like to go through this routine diminishment without ever getting used to it, the same way one never quite gets used to a night with no moon. Maybe the moon has not risen yet? Perhaps it has already set? As often as the three dark days come around, it is easy to forget them. Yet they are part of the natural way of things, as predictable as the tides.

In 2009 I visited Notre Dame de Chartres for the first time. It had been on my radar for years by then, not only because it is one of the most stunning Gothic cathedrals in Europe but also because of the huge labyrinth in its nave, which has drawn pilgrims to Chartres since the twelfth century. Before that, they came to view the *Sancta Camisa,* brought to Chartres by Charles the Bald in 876. According to sacred legend, it is the shawl worn by Mary while she was giving birth to Jesus.

I did not care about the shawl. I wanted to see the flying buttresses, the carvings over the doors, the stained glass windows, and above all the labyrinth. A friend of mine had gone there years earlier to walk it, but when she entered the church she could not find it. Walking past rows of chairs on her way to the altar, she was stopped halfway down the aisle by a sudden heaviness in her feet. Looking down, she saw that she was standing in the exact center of the labyrinth, which was completely covered by chairs. It turned out that the cathedral clergy were tired of all the tourists who came only for the labyrinth and not for the Catholic mass, so they kept the space set up for services during the week and uncovered the labyrinth only on Fridays.

Before I entered the cathedral for the first time, I stood outside and looked up at the famously mismatched towers that flanked the front door. The north tower looked like a wedding cake, with one frilly arch stacked on another all the way up to the flaming sun symbol at the top. The south tower was both shorter and plainer, a steep pyramid with a new moon symbol at the top. Later I would discover the symbolism of these two towers, apparent only to students of sacred geometry. While some credit the Knights Templar with the genius of the plan, anyone can do the math.

If you sketch the front of the cathedral on a piece of tracing paper and lay it over a sketch of the interior, you can see that the sun tower fits perfectly inside the cathedral. With its base resting on the first step into the church, the tip of its spire just touches the wall behind the altar. The sun tower measures 365 feet from end to end, one foot for each day of the year. The moon tower is exactly 28 feet shorter—minus one foot for each lunar cycle of the year—so that its tip rests lower, in the exact center of the apse.

As if that were not enough, the rose window that dominates the façade of the church and the labyrinth on the floor inside are both forty feet in diameter—perfect twins in size and placement If you could lower the front wall of the church gently to the floor, the window that channels the light would fit right over the labyrinth that covers the darkness. The number of stones in the labyrinth is the number of days a full-term baby spends in its mother's womb. In these ways and more, Chartres Cathedral is a microcosm of both the human journey from life to death and the journey of the earth around the sun, offering a concrete corrective to anyone who thinks of the physical and the spiritual as two separate things.

The labyrinth was spectacular, but I expected that. What I did not expect was the church beneath the church—the vast crypt that was undamaged by the fire of 1194 and became the footprint for the new Gothic cathedral to rise above. No one knows why there are no tombs down there, but there are none. There is an ancient well where legend says Norse invaders threw two Christians in the ninth century, but other than that, the crypt is one long mall of chapels: seven plain Romanesque ones along the sides and the Chapel of Notre Dame de Sous-Terre at the end—Our Lady of the Underground—a low, dark cavern lined with dark wood pews.

Above the altar is a small wooden statue of a Madonna and child, carved to replace the more ancient one destroyed during the French Revolution. Mother and child are both so dark that it is difficult to see them from a distance. It is only when I walk behind the altar for a closer look that I clearly see the face of the stiff woman sitting on her throne with her stiff baby on her lap. Her eyes are closed. Her son's are wide open. Neither of them is lovely, and yet they are arresting, if only because they require such careful looking to see.

Art historians count the statue among the many *Vierges noires* in France—black Virgins—so called not because their features are African or because they have gotten covered up with candle soot, but because their skin is dark. According to one theory, Mary's skin is dark because when Catholic devotion to the Virgin replaced Druidic devotion to the Goddess, Mary inherited the Goddess's dark skin. Another theory favors the identification of Mary with indigenous people. The darker she is, the more she resembles those who serve instead of those who rule. I have seen plenty of Romani women in France begging for food for their children, and Our Lady of the Underground does not look like one of them. She looks like Elinor of Aquitane, only darker.

As I continue looking at her after I return to my pew, another possibility occurs to me. The darkness is not meant to convey anything about Mary; it is meant to convey something about those of us who look at her. We see through a glass darkly. She does not care how curious we are. We can rest a flashlight right on her nose if we want, and still she will not open her eyes. No amount of light can make her give up her mystery. Earlier, in the gift shop, I saw a silver medal with her image on it and her mantra on the back. "All must come through me in order to live in the light," it read. She might as well have signed it *Our Lady of the Cave*.

There is no moonlight down here, but that is clearly her kind of light. If I want something more brightly lit, I can go upstairs and look at one of the white Virgins in the main cathedral. That is where all the tourists are anyway. Almost no one comes down here to visit Our Lady of the Underground, either because they have bad knees or because they have heard it is a crypt.

"What's down there?" I hear someone at the top of the steps ask a woman ahead of me on the way out.

"Nothing," she says. "It's dark and incredibly gloomy."

Outside again, I look up at the moon tower. Even by the full light of day, there is not much to see. Compared to the sugar-spun sun tower, the moon tower looks like a pointed hat, without a pinnacle or mullion anywhere. Its eyes are closed too.

Later, after dark, I go back to see Chartres en Lumières. The whole city is lit up, with elaborate colored designs projected on the Museum of Fine Arts, the Courtille Theatre, the Halles aux Grains, and the Médiathèque. Parents herd children from place to place, promising them ice cream at the end, while tourists snap pictures and lovers sit on benches, wrapped in each others' arms.

The largest crowd stands on the plaza in front of the cathedral, gaping at the huge Virgin covering the western façade of the church while Poulenc plays over loudspeakers. This Mary is an exact replica of the *Belle Verrière* window inside—a vividly colored version of Our Lady of the Underground. The blue of the Lady's gown is so blue and the red background behind her is so red that the colors give me a tiny headache while my eyes adjust. The sun and moon towers look almost even in this light, with identical mosaics of gold and lapis crosses projected on both. Over and over I run my eyes from the Virgin's tidy feet to the twin spires over her head, stopping when I run out of lights, to start all over again. When my neck finally gets tired, I stretch it all the way back, which is how I see what the moon tower has been pointing to all along: the real moon, hanging over Chartres with such pale white light that it is barely visible above all the hot colors below.

Looking back and forth between the two light shows in front of me, I understand the choice I am being offered: do I want the kind of light that shines *on* things or the kind that shines *from* them? The next morning I stop by the cathedral gift shop to buy the silver medal with Our Lady of the Underground on it. *All must come through me in order to live in the light.* She has been talking to me ever since.

Our Lady of the Underground never asks me to choose between day and night. If I want to flourish, I need the ever-changing light of darkness as much as I need the full light of day. *Give your heart to them both,* she says. When I complain that I cannot see as well at night as I can during the day, she tells me this is a good thing. *Maybe it will slow you down.* When I tell her that I cannot get as much done at night because darkness makes me sleepy, she says yes, that is the plan. *Maybe you will get some rest.* When I point out that slowing down just makes me think about things I would rather not think about, she laughs. *Do you think that not thinking about them will make them go away?*

She is always right.

What do you want from me? I ask her. *Nothing,* she says.

At first I think she means that she does not want anything from me, but that is not what she means. She means that she wants nothing *for* me, because she knows how scared I am of it—of being nothing, doing nothing, believing nothing, being good for nothing, ending up nothing. *Nada.* She seems to think there is more to it than that, which is why she wants it for me. If I could lean into it a little more, she says, I might be surprised. I tell her I will take it under consideration.

"The soul does not grow by addition but by subtraction," wrote the fourteenth-century mystic Meister Eckhart.

> *Leave place, leave time,*
> *Avoid even image!*
> *Go forth without a way*
> *On the narrow path,*
> *Then you will find the desert track.*[2]

According to the Gospels, Jesus knew that track well. He made a habit of sleeping outdoors under the stars—on a mountain, if he could find one. The fact that this is reported more than once without any further detail suggests that he went alone. When he took people with him, they usually had plenty to say about it afterward, but no one has anything to say about what Jesus did on those nights alone. Even his famous forty days and nights in the wilderness pass without comment until they are over, which is when he and the devil sort out who works for whom.

When you put this together with the fact that God speaks to Jesus only once in the entire New Testament—shortly after he is baptized by John—it seems clear that this father and this son were not in constant public conversation. Their conversation was almost entirely private, when Jesus went out on the mountain to spend the night with God in prayer. If Jesus was truly human, as Christians insist he was, his sleep architecture was like anyone else's. He stayed awake awhile. He slept awhile. He woke awhile later, rested a few hours, then slept some more. When he opened his eyes, he saw the night sky. When he closed them again, the sky stayed right there. The only witnesses to his most intimate moments with God were the moon and the stars—and it was all prayer.

Outside my window, the full moon has risen high in the sky, casting such strong light on the pasture that there seem to be twice as many trees as usual—the trees plus their shadows. *All must come through me to live in the light,* the lady in the moon says, and I believe her. When I wake in the morning, I will give thanks for all the bright gifts that spill forth from the *nada* of God: sunshine, warmth, and work; faith, hope, and love. What I now know for certain—perhaps the only thing I know for certain—is that while these gifts may arrive by day, they come burnished by darkness, like shoes left outside our doors for polishing while we sleep. Or better yet, like dazzling stones we have brought back from our shallow caves in the darkness of our pockets. If they do not dazzle in daylight, then what better reminder could we have?

The light was never in the stone. It was in our eyes all along.

My Lord God, I have no idea where I am going.
I do not see the road ahead of me. I cannot
know for certain where it will end. Nor do I
really know myself, and the fact that I think I
am following your will does not mean that I am
actually doing so. But I believe that the desire to
please you does in fact please you. And I hope I
have that desire in all that I am doing. I hope
that I will never do anything apart from that
desire. And I know that if I do this you will
lead me by the right road, though I may know
nothing about it. Therefore I will trust you
always though I may seem to be lost and in the
shadow of death. I will not fear, for you are ever
with me, and you will never leave me to face my
perils alone.

—Thomas Merton, *Thoughts in Solitude*

Epilogue:
Blessing the Day

Day to day pours forth speech,
and night to night declares knowledge.
—Psalm 19.2

Someday I would like to know what a book is about before writing it, but so far that has not happened. When I started writing this one, all I knew was that I needed to know more about darkness—the physical and psychological kind as well as the spiritual and theological kind. The reasons that I had been given for staying out of the dark were becoming less and less convincing as I had more and more occasions to walk in it—caring for aging parents, going to the funerals of people I loved, coping with economic crisis, seeing ice caps melt, and watching churches close—all the while weighing a bag of Christian certainties that had less in it all the time. The energy required to keep darkness at bay was fast becoming more than I could manage. Perhaps there was another way?

So here at the end, I think this may be a book about living with loss, which is tough enough in any place or time but is especially difficult in a culture that works so hard to look the other way. Type "loss management" into your favorite search engine and you will find a million sites willing to help you with that. The churches I know best would never use such language, but they have their own strategies for managing loss. Chief among these is the strategy of spiritual bypassing, which markets faith in God as protection from every kind of darkness. Walk as a child of the light, the advertisement reads, and all your nights will be bright as day. This full solar version of Christianity works so well for so many people that those of us who cannot buy it are bound to wonder what is wrong with us. I wondered what was wrong with me, anyhow, which was why I needed to know more about darkness.

Pema Chödrön did not become one of my teachers until I had almost finished writing, but she diagnosed the problem so well that I can no longer say it without her help. We are all so busy constructing zones of safety that keep breaking down, she says, that we hardly notice where all the suffering is coming from. We keep thinking that the problem is out there, in the things that scare us: dark nights, dark thoughts, dark guests, dark emotions. If we could just defend ourselves better against those things, we think, then surely we would feel more solid and secure. But of course we are wrong about that, as experience proves again and again. The real problem has far less to do with *what is really out there* than it does with our *resistance to finding out what is really out there*. The suffering comes from our reluctance to learn to walk in the dark.[1]

This is not a how-to book, but if it were, the only instruction would be to become more curious about your own darkness. What can you learn about your fear of it by staying with it for a moment before turning on the lights? Where can you feel the fear in your body? When have you felt that way before? What are you afraid is going to happen to you, and what is your mind telling you to do about it? What stories do you tell yourself to keep your fear in place? What helps you stay conscious even when you are afraid? What have you learned in the dark that you could never have learned in the light?

Most people do not get very far into this list before they want to know when they can stop. How long do they have to do this? Since this is not a how-to book, the good news is that you do not have to do it at all. But if you are ready to learn to walk in the dark, then try doing it while you take three long breaths. Next time, you can try four. After that, you can trust yourself to know when to stop and when to go. Believe me, you will know. If you have even one friend who seems less afraid of the dark than you are, ask that friend to explore the dark with you. Whether you go it alone or with company, your job is as simple and as hard as this: drop what you believe about the dark, or have been taught about the dark, to see for yourself what is true.

Whatever it is, it is bound to be different for you than for me. It is also bound to change, since endarkenment, like enlightenment, is a work in progress. The best thing I can say is that learning to walk in the dark has allowed me to take back my faith, removing it from the glare of the full solar tradition to recover by the light of the moon. Now the sun still comes up, but it also goes down. Blessing the day means accepting my full quota of light *and* of dark, even when I cannot see what I am blessing. Is this dangerous? Perhaps. At this point I am more afraid of what I might leave out instead of what I might let in. With limited time left on this earth, I want more than the top halves of things—the spirit but not the flesh, the presence but not the absence, the faith but not the doubt. This late in life, *I want it all.*

Among the other treasures of darkness I have dug up along the way are a new collection of Bible stories that all happen after dark, a new set of teachers who know their way around the dark, a deeper reverence for the cloud of unknowing, a greater ability to abide in God's absence, and—by far the most valuable of all—a fresh baptism in the truth that loss is the way of life. That last one is a hard one to trust, which is why I need to keep walking in the dark. It takes practice to keep stepping into *la noche oscura*, to keep seizing the night as well as the day.

My hope is that when the last big step comes, both my legs and my heart will know the way.

In the meantime, I am planning a moon garden in the open patch outside my kitchen window, to go with the day lilies that crowd the driveway from late spring through autumn. Moon gardens have been around a long time, though most people who plant them nowadays supplement the moonlight with cleverly hidden artificial lights that do not wax or wane. The light in my garden will wax and wane. Right now the plan includes a pagoda dogwood for height, a couple of white rose bushes and a gardenia for fragrance, maidenhair grass for rustling in the wind, and night phlox for texture. In and around all of that I will tuck as many white flowers as I can to catch the moonlight when it comes: evening primrose, angel's trumpet, gooseneck loosestrife, pearly everlasting—and moonflowers, of course.

The names are so lovely that I may just say them over and over again instead of punishing my knees with the actual planting of a garden. Then again, what better way to keep track of what phase the moon is in than to watch the light in my garden grow? And what better way—when the moon and the flowers are both full, and I go outside to walk among them—to remember how much light there is in the dark?

ACKNOWLEDGMENTS

There would be no book in your hands if people like you did not still buy books, so you belong at the top of this list. Thank you for reading this book. If you happened to buy it from an independent bookseller, I hope you will thank that person and do everything you can to help him or her stay in business. There is no substitute for being guided to good books by people we know who also know us well.

I am grateful to Mickey Maudlin, Mark Tauber, and Claudia Boutote at HarperOne for publishing this book, and to my white knight, Tom Grady, for guiding it into their hands. Cynthia Shattuck read every line of the first draft, making suggestions that significantly improved those that followed. She is the only grammarian whom I obey without question, since her intuition is as flawless as her syntax. Mickey Maudlin and Tom Grady also read early chapters of the book, seeing things I could not see and helping me bring them into much better focus.

I am also grateful to Katy Renz at HarperOne for helping me navigate the maze of publication from beginning to end with unfailing kindness, and to Mandy Chahal for maintaining a Facebook page that allows me to stay in touch with readers while I am writing. The rest of my skilled team at HarperOne includes

Laina Adler, Darcy Cohan, Terri Leonard, Michele Wetherbee, Janelle Agius, Amy VanLangen, Julie Baker, Melinda Mullin, Lisa Zuniga, Elizabeth Berg, and Kimberly McCutcheon, without whom this book would never have made it across the finish line. My deep thanks to you all.

Fran McKendree first opened the door to darkness by inviting me to join him and John Philip Newell for an Advent retreat at the Kanuga Conference Center in 2008. Many of the ideas in this book were born there and were subsequently developed for a January Adventure with Brian McLaren in 2011, the DuBose Lectures at the University of the South in 2011, and the Bowers conference at Virginia Theological Seminary in 2012. I was also greatly helped by comments and questions from those who listened to early chapters of the book at Davidson College and at Church of the Holy Spirit in Orleans, Massachusetts. In addition to those already named, I am grateful to my gracious hosts at those places, including William Stafford, Christopher Bryan, and Bill Brosend at Sewanee's School of Theology; Ian Markham, Barney Hawkins, and Shelagh Casey-Brown at Virginia Theological Seminary; Robert Spach at Davidson; Adam Linton and Sarah Kelb at Holy Spirit; and Buzzy Pickren at January Adventure.

Rockwell and Marrion Ward are the heroes of chapter 6. They not only led me safely into Organ Cave and back out again; they also proofread the chapter for accuracy. Any errors that remain are mine alone. Rockwell, by the way, is also the astronomer who first told me the story of Cassiopeia.

From the minute Lauren Winner learned about this project, she sent me books that were exactly what I needed. I am grateful to her not only for these permanent additions to my lunar library but also for the gifts of her writing and friendship. Ken Sehested also sent me an essay he wrote, called "*Carpe Noctem:* Spiritual Vision for Living in Dark Times," which encouraged me to seize the night. My friends Martha Sterne and Judy Barber have listened to me talk about this book for years without ever blocking my calls. My thanks to them both for their lasting friendship and generosity of soul.

Finally, I am grateful to Ed, who remains my best reader and best friend. He watched stars, played word games, did research, and remembered stories with me. He listened to me talk about darkness until his cup runneth over. Then he spent lots of time alone, handling all the chores on two continents while I finished this book. I cannot imagine anything without him. My thanks and love to Ed.

Barbara Brown Taylor
Ballyferriter, Ireland
June 2013

NOTES

Chapter 1: Who's Afraid of the Dark?

1. Lisa Belkin, "Are Fairy Tales Too Scary for Children?" *New York Times,* January 12, 2009.
2. James Bremner, "Fear of the Night," in *Let There Be Night,* ed. Paul Bogard (Reno: University of Nevada Press, 2008), 184.

Chapter 2: The Fear of the Lord

1. *The Cloud of Unknowing,* ed. Emilie Griffin (San Francisco: HarperSanFrancisco, 1981), 15.
2. *Commentary on the Song of Songs, Homily 11,* quoted by Philip Kariatlis in "Dazzling Darkness: The Mystic or Theophanic Theology of Saint Gregory of Nyssa," *Phronema* 27, no. 2 (2012): 99–123.

Chapter 3: Hampered by Brilliance

1. Verlyn Klinkenborg, "Our Vanishing Night," *National Geographic* (November 2008), 102–123.
2. James Agee and Walker Evans, *Let Us Now Praise Famous Men* (Boston: Houghton Mifflin, 1988), 211.
3. Christopher Dewdney, *Acquainted with the Night* (Toronto: HarperPerennialCanada, 2004), 210.
4. Dewdney, *Acquainted with the Night,* 178.
5. Chet Raymo, *The Soul of the Night* (Cambridge MA: Cowley Publications, 1992), 57.
6. Raymo, *The Soul of the Night,* 84.
7. "Brain Basics: Understanding Sleep," National Institute of Neurological Disorders and Stroke, accessed December 26, 2012, www.ninds.nih.gov/disorders/brain_basics/understanding_sleep.htm.
8. Dewdney, *Acquainted with the Night,* 109.
9. Dewdney, *Acquainted with the Night,* 104; Christina Robertson, "Circadian Heart," in *Let There Be Night,* ed. Paul Bogard, 175.
10. Jane Brox, *Brilliant* (New York: Houghton Mifflin Harcourt, 2010), 303.

Chapter 4: The Dark Emotions

1. Mirium Greenspan, "The Wisdom in Dark Emotions," *Shambhala Sun* (January 2003), 58.
2. Mirium Greenspan, *Healing Through the Dark Emotions* (Boston: Shambhala, 2004), xiv.
3. Greenspan, *Healing Through the Dark Emotions,* 1.
4. Ken Wilber, *One Taste* (Boston: Shambhala, 2000), 27.

Chapter 5: The Eyes of the Blind

1. Diane Ackerman, *A Natural History of the Senses* (New York: Random House. 1990), 230.
2. "Blind Leading the Blind," on Jacqueline Harmon Butler's website, accessed October 15, 2012, www.jacquelineharmonbutler.com/BLTB_Switzerland.cfm.
3. "Opaque—Dining in the Dark," Yelp.com, accessed October 15, 2012, www.yelp.com/biz/opaque-dining-in-the-dark-at-v-lounge-santa-monica.
4. "Opaque—Dining in the Dark."
5. Annie Dillard, *Pilgrim at Tinker's Creek* (New York: Harper's Magazine Press, 1974), 28.
6. Dialogue in the Dark website, accessed January 1, 2013, www.dialogue-in-the-dark.com.
7. *The Book of Common Prayer* (New York: Church Hymnal Corporation, 1986), 133.
8. Jacques Lusseyran, *Against the Pollution of the I* (Sandpoint, ID: Morning Light Press, 2006), 31.
9. Lusseyran, *Against the Pollution of the I,* 27–28.
10. Lusseyran, *Against the Pollution of the I,* 65.
11. Lusseyran, *Against the Pollution of the I,* 83.
12. John 9:39.

Chapter 6: Entering the Stone

1. "John Cage quotations," University of Pennsylvania website, accessed November 23, 2012, www.english.upenn.edu/~afilreis/88/cage-quotes.html.
2. Barbara Hurd, *Entering the Stone* (New York: Houghton Mifflin, 2003), 133.
3. Hurd, *Entering the Stone,* 136.

Chapter 7: The Dark Night of the Soul

1. Gerald G. May, *The Dark Night of the Soul* (San Francisco: HarperOne, 2005), 34.
2. Karen Armstrong, *The Great Transformation* (New York: Anchor, 2007).
3. Phyllis Tickle, *The Great Awakening* (Grand Rapids: Baker Books, 2008).
4. Harvey Cox, *The Future of Faith* (San Francisco: HarperOne, 2009), 7.
5. James Fowler, *Stages of Faith* (San Francisco: HarperOne, 1981).
6. Peter Rollins, *The Fidelity of Betrayal* (Brewster, MA: Paraclete Press, 2008), 113.
7. May, *The Dark Night of the Soul,* 61.
8. Denys Turner, *The Darkness of God* (Cambridge: Cambridge University Press, 1995), 243–44.
9. May, *The Dark Night of the Soul,* 94.

Chapter 8: Working with Darkness

1. Clark Strand, "Turn Out the Lights," *Tricycle: The Buddhist Review* 19, no. 3 (Spring 2010): 42.
2. *The Merck Manual of Medical Information, Home Edition,* ed. Robert Berkow (Whitehouse Station, NJ: Merck Research Laboratories, 1997), 1248.
3. Dewdney, *Acquainted with the Night,* 294.

Chapter 9: Our Lady of the Underground

1. *The Book of Common Prayer,* 880.
2. Bernard McGinn, *The Mystical Thought of Meister Eckhart* (New York: Crossroad, 2001), 114.

Epilogue: Blessing the Day

1. If you do not already know Pema Chödrön's work, you can start almost anywhere. She uses some of this language in *The Places That Scare You* (Boston: Shambhala, 2005) and some more of it in *Taking the Leap* (Boston: Shambhala, 2012).

Sources

Ackerman, Diane. *A Natural History of the Senses.* New York: Random House, 1990.

Agee, James, and Walker Evans. *Let Us Now Praise Famous Men: Three Tenant Families.* Boston: Houghton Mifflin, 1988.

Armstrong, Karen. *The Great Transformation: The Beginning of Our Religious Traditions.* New York: Anchor, 2007.

Attlee, James. *Nocturne: A Journey in Search of Moonlight.* Chicago: University of Chicago Press, 2011.

Bogard, Paul, ed. *The End of Night: Searching for Natural Darkness in an Age of Artificial Light.* New York: Little, Brown and Company, 2013.

———. *Let There Be Night: Testimony on Behalf of the Dark.* Reno: University of Nevada Press, 2008.

Brox, Jane. *Brilliant: The Evolution of Artificial Light.* New York: Houghton Mifflin Harcourt, 2010.

Brunner, Bernd. *Moon: A Brief History.* New Haven, CT: Yale University Press, 2010.

Caldwell, Mark. *New York Night: The Mystique and Its History.* New York: Scribner, 2005.

Chödrön, Pema. *Taking the Leap.* Boston: Shambhala, 2012.

———. *The Places That Scare You.* Boston: Shambhala, 2005.

The Cloud of Unknowing with the Book of Privy Counsel. Translated by Carmen Acevedo Butcher. Boston: Shambhala, 2009.

Cox, Harvey. *The Future of Faith*. San Francisco: HarperOne, 2009.

Dewdney, Christopher. *Acquainted with the Night: Excursions Through the World after Dark*. Toronto: HarperPerennialCanada, 2004.

Dillard, Annie. *Pilgrim at Tinker Creek*. New York: Harper's Magazine Press, 1974.

Ekirch, A. Roger. *At Day's Close: Night in Times Past*. New York: W. W. Norton, 2005.

Fowler, James. *Stages of Faith: The Psychology of Human Development and the Quest for Meaning*. New York: HarperCollins, 1981.

Greenspan, Miriam. *Healing Through the Dark Emotions*. Boston: Shambhala, 2004.

Griffin, Emilie, ed. *The Cloud of Unknowing*. San Francisco: HarperSanFrancisco, 1981.

Hurd, Barbara. *Entering the Stone: On Caves and Feeling Through the Dark*. New York: Houghton Mifflin, 2003.

John of the Cross. *Dark Night of the Soul*. Translated and edited by E. Allison Peers. New York: Image Books/Doubleday, 2005 (1959).

Kariatlis, Philip. "Dazzling Darkness: The Mystic or Theophanic Theology of Saint Gregory of Nyssa." *Phronema* 27, no. 2 (2012): 99–123.

Klinkenborg, Verlyn. "Our Vanishing Night." *National Geographic* (November 2008): 102–23.

Lusseyran, Jacques. *Against the Pollution of the I: Selected Writings of Jacques Lusseyran*. Sandpoint, ID: Morning Light Press, 2006.

———. *And There Was Light: Autobiography of Jacques Lusseyran, Blind Hero of the French Resistance*. Translated by Elizabeth R. Cameron. Sandpoint, ID: Morning Light Press, 2006.

May, Gerald G. *The Dark Night of the Soul: A Psychiatrist Explores the Connection Between Darkness and Spiritual Growth*. New York: HarperOne, 2005.

McGinn, Bernard. *The Mystical Thought of Meister Eckhart: The Man from Whom God Hid Nothing*. New York: Crossroad, 2001.

Melbin, Murray. *Night as Frontier: Colonizing the World after Dark*. New York: Free Press, 1987.

Moore, Thomas. *Dark Nights of the Soul*. New York: Gotham, 2004.

Raymo, Chet. *The Soul of the Night: An Astronomical Pilgrimage*. Cambridge, MA: Cowley Publications, 1992.

Rollins, Peter. *The Fidelity of Betrayal: Towards a Church Beyond Belief*. Brewster, MA: Paraclete Press, 2008.

Saint-Exupéry, Antoine de. *Night Flight*. New York: Harcourt, 1932.

Schrock, Daniel P. *The Dark Night: A Gift of God*. Scottdale, PA: Herald Press, 2009.

Simmons, Philip. *Learning to Fall: The Blessings of an Imperfect Life*. New York: Bantam, 2002.

Stevenson, Robert Louis. *Travels with a Donkey*. New York: Atlas, 2008.

Strand, Clark. "Turn Out the Lights." *Tricycle: The Buddhist Review* 19, no. 3 (Spring 2010): 40–49.

Styron, William. *Darkness Visible: A Memoir of Madness*. New York: Random House, 1990.

Thoreau, Henry David. *Night and Moonlight*. New York: Hubert Rutherford Brown, 1921.

Tickle, Phyllis. *The Great Awakening: How Christianity Is Changing and Why*. Grand Rapids, MI: Baker Books, 2008.

Turner, Denys. *The Darkness of God: Negativity in Christian Mysticism.* Cambridge: Cambridge University Press, 1995.

Wilber, Ken. *One Taste: Daily Reflections on Integral Spirituality.* Boston: Shambhala, 2000.

Wiman, Christian. *My Bright Abyss.* New York: Farrar, Straus and Giroux, 2013.